Hand-Drawn Renderings of Architecture and Interior Design

Design Inspiration and Visual Reference of Illustration Techniques

Rick Bartholomew

PAGE PUBLISHING, INC.
Conneaut Lake, PA

First originally published by Page Publishing 2021

ISBN 978-1-6624-3792-2 (pbk)
ISBN 978-1-6624-3793-9 (digital)

Printed in the United States of America

Contents

Preface

This book is a collection of architectural and interior design illustration plates to foster inspiration of technique for students in programs of design as a visual reference in building upon one's skills in hand-drawn rendering composition. It is also hoped that design professionals can use these plates to enhance their rendering skills and visual references for projects, and the home building industry could utilize the collection to initiate design discussions with potential clients.

There is a "soft" movement within the various design disciplines, their clients, and higher educational institutions to once again appreciate and embrace hand-drawn illustrations. The book of plates is a compilation of residential and nonresidential pen-and-ink and colored renderings of exterior and interior design that the author has created over his tenure of professional practice not only in Oklahoma but also across the US.

The intent is to convey a collection of illustrations with a limited amount of written text to just show technique with only bullet-point notes on each plate. Client credits and permissions to publish are included in the appendix.

The illustration plates were created either in pen and ink and/or colored marker with colored pencil highlights. The author has also used acrylic paints to accentuate reflective highlights and detailed landscape and planting features, which adds color intensity and vibrancy to illustration techniques. The quality of any illustration depends on the understanding and skill at creating two- and three-dimensional constructed line drawings prior to applying material delineation, color, shades, and shadows.

There are many excellent how-to publications that are great in building those constructed line drawings and step-by-step color applications; but this book of plates is to inspire finished detail, design style, and composition. One can use the book as a design inspiration for one's future projects and clients.

Acknowledgments

I would like to extend a grateful thank-you and professional support to the following clients and companies for the wonderful opportunities extended to me in creating their visions through my illustration techniques.

In addition, sketching and rendering workshops that I conducted for students of design and firms have fostered opportunities to extend my portfolios and promote the art of hand-drawn illustrations.

Ambler Architects (Bartlesville, Oklahoma)
Bainbridge Design Group (Tulsa, Oklahoma)
Brian D. Wiggs Homes, Inc. (Jenks, Oklahoma)
Customs by Vaughn (Owasso, Oklahoma)
Duvall Atelier (Tulsa, Oklahoma)
Ferrell Building Products (Tulsa, Oklahoma)
George Beltz (Steelville, Missouri)
Henk-Seng Design, LLC (Tulsa, OK)
Jamie Birks (Tulsa, Oklahoma
Jane Swinney (Stillwater, Oklahoma)
Jerald Vahn Willis Designs (New York City)
June Gilliam (Stillwater, Oklahoma [formerly Es Posible, Scottsdale, Arizona])
Kitchen Concepts (Lynn Knight Jessee) (Tulsa, Oklahoma)
Kappa Kappa Iota (Tulsa, Oklahoma)
Kinslow, Keith, and Todd, Inc. (Tulsa, Oklahoma)
KSQ Architects (Tulsa, Oklahoma)
Mel Bean Interiors (Tulsa, Oklahoma)

Merritt Properties (Santa Barbara, California)
New Line Skate Parks, Inc. (San Diego, California)
SKS (Huntington Beach, California)
Steve White (Disney, Oklahoma)
Suanne Blair (Tulsa, Oklahoma)
Tom Little Construction (Coweta, Oklahoma)
WSB Homes

Section 1

Residential Exterior Elevations

Plate 1. Country French in brick, stone, and wood shingle siding wood shutter accents. Medium is colored marker with colored pencil and acrylic paint plant accents.

Plate 2. Country French in brick, stone, and wood siding and shutter accents. Medium is colored marker with colored pencil and acrylic paint plant accents.

Plate 3. Modern farmhouse in board and batten siding, standing seam roof accents, and brick.
Medium is colored marker with colored pencil and acrylic paint plant accents.

Plate 4. Modern farmhouse in board and batten siding, brick, and standing seam metal roofing. Medium is colored marker with colored pencil and acrylic paint plant accents.

Plate 5. Country French in brick, stone, board and batten wood siding, and shutter accents. Medium is colored marker with colored pencil and acrylic paint plant accents.

Plate 6. Ranch in brick, wood siding, composition shingles, and standing metal seam roofing.
Medium is colored marker with colored pencil and acrylic paint plant accents.

Plate 7. Country French in brick, stone, and wood lap shingle siding and shutter accents. Medium is colored marker with colored pencil and acrylic paint plant accents.

Plate 8. Country French in pen-and-ink version of Plate 7. Fading finish materials give the illusion of natural light accents and create surface variation.

Plate 9. Modern English Tudor in stucco finish, wood lap garage doors, and standing seam metal roof accents. Medium is colored marker with colored pencil and acrylic paint plant accents.

Plate 10. Modern English Tudor in pen-and-ink version of plate 9

Plate 11. Transitional in stucco finish, stone, diagonal wood slat garage doors, wood shake shingles, and standing seam metal roof accents. Medium is colored marker with colored pencil and acrylic paint plant accents.

Plate 12. Transitional in pen and ink version of plate 11

Plate 13. Modern farmhouse in stucco finish, stone, glass garage doors, board and batten chimneys, wood shake shingles, and standing seam metal roof accents. Medium is colored marker with colored pencil and acrylic paint plant accents.

Plate 14. Postmodern in Dryvit wall finish, vertical metal siding, stained wood garage doors, metal roofing shingles, and iron railing accents. Medium is colored marker with colored pencil.

Plate 15. Modern cottage in stucco, stone, concrete, irregular cut lap siding, natural timber roof supports, metal standing seam ridge panels and chimney hats, and diamond-shaped slate roofing. Medium is pen and ink with colored marker and pencil.

Plate 16. Modern cottage in pen-and-ink version of plate 15

Plate 17. French transitional in brick, composition shingles, wood window header accents, and multipaned windows. Medium is colored marker with colored pencil and acrylic paint plant accents.

Plate 18. Colonial in wood lap siding, composition shingles, bay windows, and window shutters. Medium is dry and wet watercolor techniques.

Plate 19. Traditional in brick, wood lap siding, composition shingles, and wood panel garage doors. Medium is dry and wet watercolor techniques.

Plate 20. Mediterranean Revival in brick, clay tile shingles, arched terra-cotta, and glass window transoms. Medium is pen and ink and heavy delineation with foliage, shades, and shadows.

Plate 21. Mediterranean Revival in less foliage delineation and shades and shadows to see more of home facade detailing of plate 20

Plate 22. Contemporary (*top left and right*) in stucco with wood lap siding. Bottom *Left:* Stucco, brick, and wood bottom lap siding. Bottom *Right:* Stucco, brick, and wood panel garage doors. Medium is pen and ink (*top left*). All others are colored marker with colored pencil and acrylic paint plant accents.

Plate23. Transitional in brick, wood lap siding, and composition shingles. Medium is colored marker and colored pencil.

Medium is quality photocopy in gray tones.

Plate 24. Tudor in stone, wood panel siding, and composition shingles. Medium is colored marker and colored pencil with acrylic paint accents.

Plate 25. Farmhouse in brick, wood board and batten panel siding, wood shake shingles, and metal standing seam roofing awnings. Medium is colored marker and colored pencil with acrylic paint accents.

Plate 26. Modern farmhouse in brick, wood board and batten panel siding, wood shake shingles, and metal standing seam roofing awnings with wood supports. Medium is colored marker and colored pencil with acrylic paint accents.

Plate 27. Mediterranean Revival in brick, wood lap board siding, composition shingles, and ironwork detailing Medium is pen and ink with nondelineated landscaping.

Plate 28. Contemporary Southwest pueblo in stucco, stone, and patina metal siding. Medium is partial pen and ink with nondelineated landscaping and colored marker with colored pencil accents.

Plate 29. Storybook cottage in wood board and batten siding, stucco, patina diamond metal tile roofing, and metal standing seam side porch roofing. Medium is pen and ink with partial colored marker and colored pencil accents.

Plate 30. English Tudor in brick, and composition shingles. Medium is pen and ink.

Section 2

Residential 3D Exterior Perspectives

Plate 31. Modern farmhouse in stone, vertical wood board and batten siding, and metal standing seam roofing. Medium is colored marker with colored pencil and acrylic paint plant accents.

Plate 32. Modern art deco in brick with cast stone accents, glass block, cast bronze window framing, bevel glass transoms, and wrought iron detailing. Medium is colored marker with colored pencil.

Plate 33. French Eclectic in stone with cast stone accents, bevel glass transoms, and steep pitched roof. Medium is pen-and-ink version of plate 34.

Plate 34. French Revival in stone with cast stone accents, bevel glass transoms, and steep pitched roof. Medium is colored marker and acrylic paint landscaping accents.

Plate 35. Contemporary in metal standing seam roof, linear stone, and divided glass window transoms. Medium is pen-and-ink version of plate 36.

Plate 36. Contemporary in metal standing seam roof, linear stone, and divided glass window transoms.
Medium is colored marker, colored pencil, and acrylic paint landscaping accents.

Plate 37. Jacobean Revival in brick, cast stone blocks and detailing, corner quoining extended wall parapets with spires, low roof balustrades, arched doorways, and bevel glass window components. Medium is pen-and-ink version of plate 38.

Plate 38. Jacobean Revival in brick, cast stone blocks and detailing, corner quoining extended wall parapets with spires, low roof balustrades, arched doorways, and bevel glass window components. Medium is colored marker, colored pencil, and acrylic paint landscaping accents.

Plate 39. French Eclectic in high-pitched roof with eaves flared outward, conical central entry tower with stepped brick detailing, dormers, and flared wing walls in brick. Medium is colored marker, colored pencil, and acrylic paint landscaping accents.

Plate 40. French Eclectic in high-pitched roof with eaves flared outward, conical central entry tower with stepped brick detailing, dormers, and flared wing walls in brick. Medium is pen-and-ink version of plate 39.

Plate 41. Modern ranch in metal standing seam hip roof with eaves flared outward, large divided glass windows, stone, vertical board and batten siding, and garage roof ridge detailing. Medium is pen and ink with gray colored marker accents/shading.

Plate 42. Colonial Revival in metal standing seam hip roof with eaves flared outward, large divided glass windows, stone, vertical board and batten siding, and garage roof ridge detailing. Medium is pen and ink.

Plate 43. Ranch in stone, vertical wood lap siding, and extended entry carport with large timber structure. Medium is pen and ink.

Plate 44. Southwest traditional in stucco exterior finishes, terra-cotta roof tiles, timber window/eave accent detailing, tapered chimney structure, ironwork detailing, and Spanish building influences. Medium is pen and ink.

Plate 45. Traditional ranch in horizontal wood lap siding, roof dormers, wrapping porch surround, and simple ridge roof. Medium is pen and ink.

Plate 46. Art moderne in smooth stucco exterior wall finish, curved corners, horizontal balustrade elements, and asymmetrical facade, sometimes glass block elements

Plate 47. Contemporary in flat cave overhang, large modular pane windows, and stucco exterior finish

Plate 48. French Norman in high-pitched roofs, stone, steep roof dormers, and arched entry doorway

Medium of all three plates is pen and ink.

Plate 49. Prairie school/textile block in flat roof, extended floor levels, modular window panels/detailing, and vertical visual emphasis. Medium is pen and ink with charcoal pencil shading.

Plate 50. Spanish Revival in flat roof with parapet walls, red-tiled shed roofs, elaborated chimney tops, intersecting tower, stucco or tile vents, and little or no eave overhangs. Medium is pen and ink.

Plate 51. Millennium/new traditional in nonemphasized detailing, simplistic to complex rooflines, stone surfacing, slate roofing shingles, and tall vertical appearance windows. Medium is pen and ink.

Plate 52. French Eclectic in steeply pitched hip roof, stone and stucco cladding, prominent stair tower with high conical roof, flared-out eaves, and gabled through-the-cornice dormer windows. Medium is pen and ink.

Medium is colored marker, colored pencil, and acrylic paint landscaping accents.

Plate 53. Modern ranch in metal standing seam hip roof with eaves flared outward, large divided glass windows, stone, vertical board and batten siding, and garage roof ridge detailing. Medium is colored marker and colored pencil and acrylic paint landscaping accents. Plate 41 is pen-and-ink version.

Section 3

Nonresidential Exterior Elevations and 3D Perspectives

Plate 54. Spanish Revival in stucco, stone, low-pitched roof, minimal eave overhang, prominent arches, and red tile roof covering. Medium is pen and ink and colored marker/colored pencil.

Plate 55. Variations on art moderne/art deco in smooth stucco, tiling, flat roof, horizontal grooves/lines on walls, horizontal emphasis asymmetrical façade, and geometric motifs. Medium is pen and ink and black marker.

Plate 56. Eclectic in brick, flat/low pitched roof, columns, detailing mix. Medium is colored marker and colored pencil with black marker.

Plate 57. Public spaces. Medium is colored marker and colored pencil with black marker.

Plate 58. Public spaces. Medium is colored marker and colored pencil with black marker and acrylic paint landscaping accents.

Neoclassical federal in Ionic Greek columns, cornice emphasized with dentil detailing, double-hung windows, fanlight detailing over windows/doors, cornice-like balustrade, and iron balcony detailing

Spanish Revival in low-pitched red tile roofing, minimal eave overhangs, arched door openings, stucco wall surfaces, towers, and arcades

Plate 59. Public buildings. Medium is pen and ink.

Greek Revival in elaborate entablature/
pediment detailing, brick/stone
module units, and stone statues

Collage of four drawing types of following pages

Art deco in chevron and stylized geometric
detailing and vertical emphasis

Plate 60. Public buildings. Medium is pen and ink.

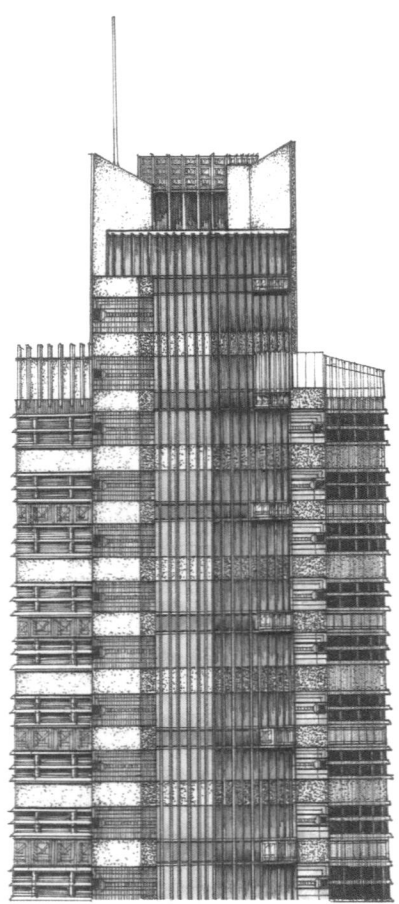

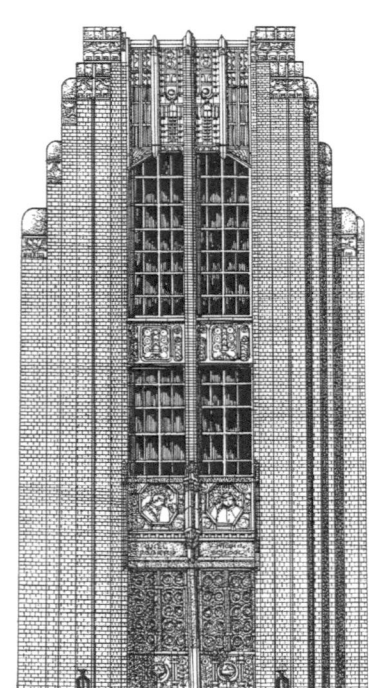

Architectural style—Wrightian

Architectural style—neoclassical with simple geometry, symmetry, and roof cornice detailing

Architectural style—art deco with vertical emphasis

Plate 61. Public buildings. Medium is pen and ink.

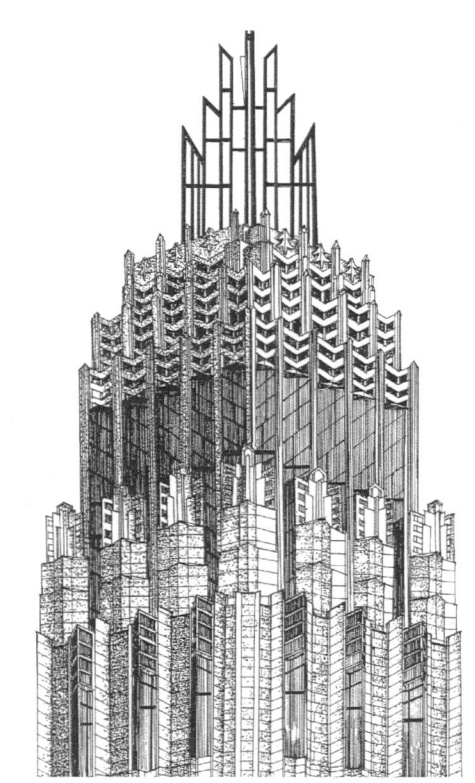

Architectural style—art deco with vertical emphasis
and chevron detailing patterns in window and facade

Architectural style—Chicago
school (Sullivanesque)

Architectural style—art deco
with vertical emphasis

Plate 62. Public buildings. Medium is pen and ink.

Architectural style—art deco with vertical emphasis and geometric terra-cotta and cast stone detailing and brick surface cladding

Architectural style—postmodern in a mix of materials, reflective materials, and complexity of composition

Plate 63. Public buildings. Medium is pen and ink.

Section 4

Interior Elevations

Design Style Descriptions for Plates 64 to 72

Art deco: the use of zigzags, chevrons, and other geometric motifs; decorative tiles; vibrant colors mixed with sliver, chrome, and black (but softer palettes of beige and creams are used)

Art nouveau: natural materials and organic forms; asymmetrical compositions; curves and soft round lines; floral motifs; muted colors of mustard, sage green, olive green, and browns with accents of lilac, violet, purples, and peacock blue

Contemporary: neutral palettes, minimalistic, clean lines, accent with metals and some wood tones, simplistic geometry

American Victorian: Darker painted and varnished woodwork; stenciling and faux arts; wall covering patterns and color schemes influenced by exotic tapestries, sometimes medieval or Gothic in nature, and usually one main color scheme with companion colors

Contemporary industrial: inspired by old factories and industrial spaces; "stripped-back" architecture; weathered-looking surfaces; raw materials such as exposed steel, brick, wood, industrial light fixtures, and cabling

Art moderne: an international style of the 1930s art deco, streamlined/aerodynamic elements, horizontal emphasis, and curving forms/details

Postmodern: rebellion against minimalist ideas of modern design, emphasis on playfulness, artsy, overstated, deconstructivism, use of vibrant colors a lot of times

Transitional: interplay of traditional and contemporary furniture, finishes, materials and fabrics, simple lines but sophisticated

Plate 64. Art deco built-ins and fireplace wall. Medium is pen and ink with colored marker, colored pencil, and white pencil highlights.

Design style—art nouveau

Design style—contemporary

Plate 65. Various kitchen cabinet styles. Medium is pen and ink with colored marker, colored pencil, and white acrylic paint highlights.

Design style: contemporary

Design style: contemporary

Plate 66. Various contemporary kitchen cabinet elevations. Medium is pen and ink with colored marker, colored pencil, and white acrylic paint highlights.

Design style—contemporary

Design style—American Victorian

Plate 67. Various built-in cabinet elevations. Medium is pen and ink with colored marker, colored pencil, and white acrylic paint highlights.

Design style—contemporary

Design style—American Craftsman

A ELEVATION CUT THRU BAR/BATHROOM

B ELEVATION AT STAIR/HALLWAY WALL

Plate 68. Contemporary industrial-style loft elevations. Medium is pen and ink with colored marker, colored pencil, and white acrylic paint highlights.

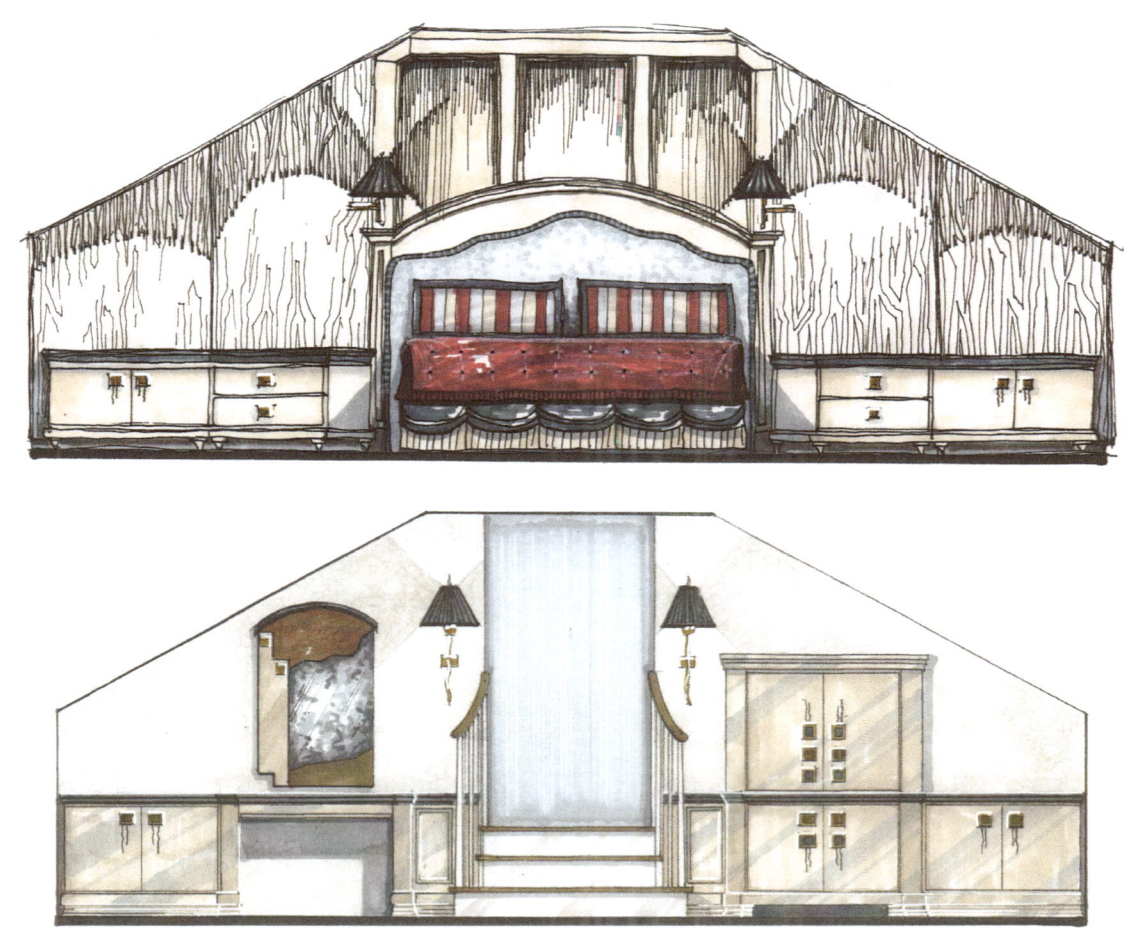

Plate 69. Art deco-style master bedroom suite elevations. Medium is pen and ink with colored marker, colored pencil, and white acrylic paint highlights.

Plate 70. Art moderne-style diner elevation. Medium is pen and ink with colored marker, colored pencil, and white acrylic paint highlights.

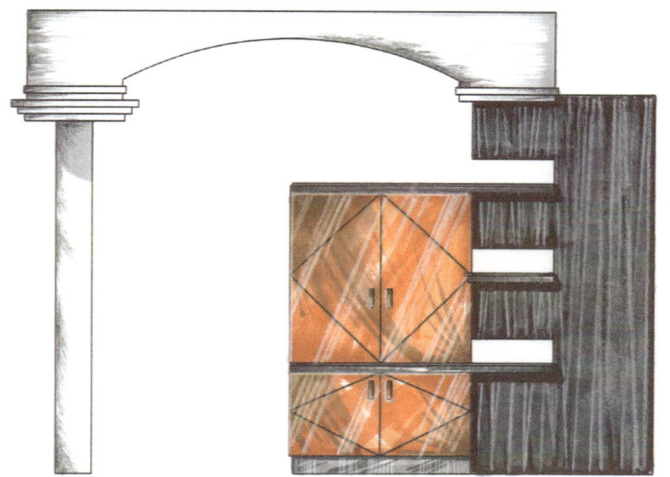

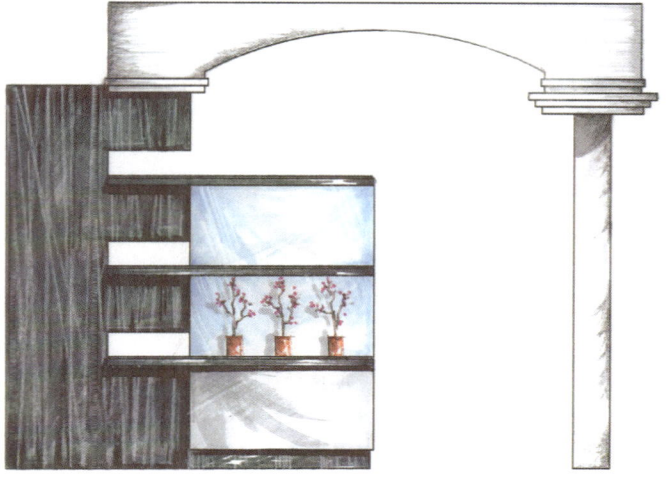

Plate 71. Postmodern room divider wall elevations. Medium is colored marker, colored pencil, and white pencil highlights.

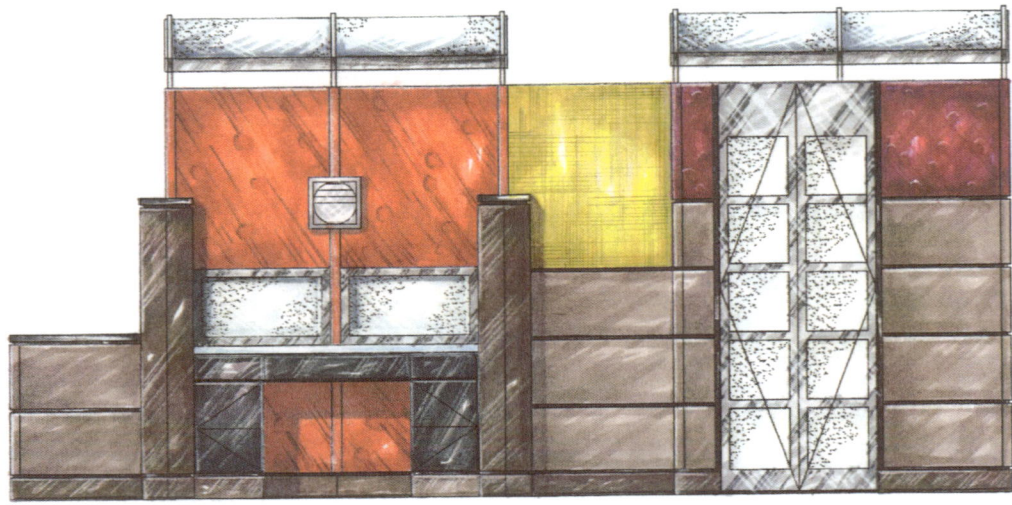

Design style—contemporary

Plate 72. Open office systems space divider elevations. Medium is colored marker, colored pencil, and white pencil highlights.

Design style—transitional

Section 5

3D Interior Illustrations

Design Style Descriptions for Plates 73 to 127

Art deco: the use of zigzags, chevrons, and other geometric motifs; decorative tiles; vibrant colors mixed with silver, chrome, and black (but softer palettes of beige and creams are used)

Art nouveau: natural materials and organic forms; asymmetrical compositions; curves and soft round lines; floral motifs; muted colors of mustard, sage green, olive green, and browns with accents of lilac, violet, purples, and peacock blue

Contemporary: neutral palettes, minimalistic, clean lines, accent with metals and some wood tones, simplistic geometry.

American Victorian: darker painted and varnished woodwork; stenciling and faux arts; wall covering patterns and color schemes influenced by exotic tapestries, sometimes medieval or Gothic in nature, and usually one main color scheme with companion colors

Contemporary industrial: inspired by old factories and industrial spaces; "stripped-back" architecture; weathered-looking surfaces; raw materials such as exposed steel, brick, and wood; industrial light fixtures; cabling

Art moderne: an international style of the 1930s art deco, streamlined/aerodynamic elements, horizontal emphasis, and curving forms/details

Postmodern: rebellion against minimalist ideas of modern design, emphasis on playfulness, artsy, overstated, deconstructivism, a lot of times use of vibrant colors

Transitional: the interplay of traditional and contemporary furniture, finishes, materials, and fabrics; simple lines but sophisticated

Country French: simplistic elegance, pop of old-world charm, shapely mirrors, weathered finishes, more neutral color palettes

Modern farmhouse: emphasizing comfort and casual living, contemporary reflection of today's styles, natural but refined eclectic sophistication

Bungalow/Craftsman: simple of form; local materials; visible handicrafts and craftsmanship; flat and square edge detailing; use of wood and stone

Contemporary Southwest: metal and wood detailing, a mix of American and Spanish traditions, high ceilings with wood beams, warm colors with accents of bright colors reflecting sky and desert, decorative accents of art, pottery, rustic furnishings, and wall textures.

Traditional: cozy/comfortable, detailed woodwork, carved moldings, sturdy period-style furnishings.

Preliminary pen-and-ink sketch, two-point perspective

Plate 73. Transitional-style dining room. Medium is colored marker, colored pencil, and white pencil highlights.

Preliminary pen-and-ink sketch, one-point perspective

Plate 74. Transitional-style gathering room. Medium is colored
marker, colored pencil, and white pencil highlights.

Preliminary pencil-line "block-out" sketch, two-point perspective

Plate 75. Country French-style kitchen. Medium is colored marker, colored pencil, and white pencil highlights.

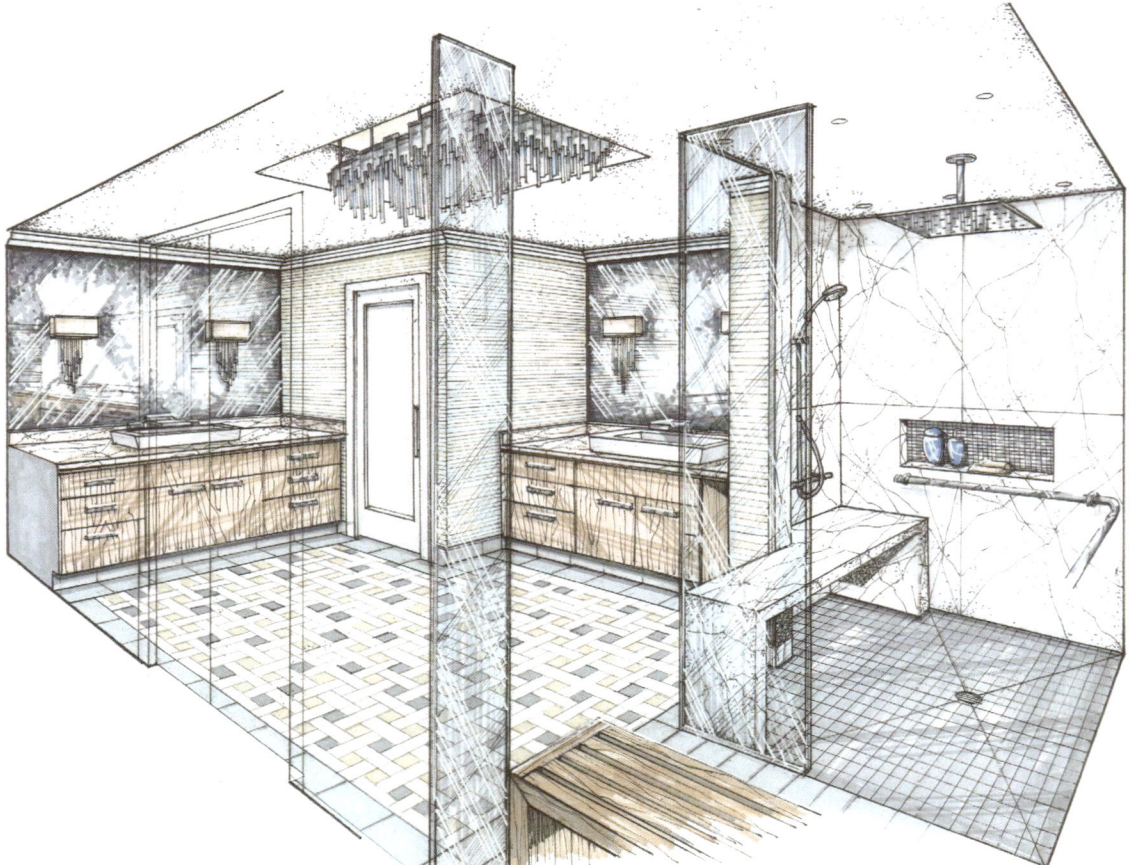

Plate 76. Contemporary-style master bath. Medium is colored marker, colored pencil, and white pencil/acrylic paint highlights.

Preliminary pencil-line "block-out" sketch, two-point perspective

Preliminary pen-and-ink sketch, two-point perspective

Preliminary pen-and-ink sketch, two-point perspective

Plate 77. Transitional-style master bath version of plate 76. Medium is colored marker, colored pencil, and white pencil/acrylic paint highlights.

Preliminary pencil-line sketch, two-point perspective

Plate 78. Contemporary-style master bath. Medium
is colored marker and colored pencil.

Preliminary pencil-line "block-out" sketch, two-point perspective

Medium in version 1 is colored marker and colored pencil with white pencil highlights.

Plate 79. Traditional-style kitchen

Medium in version 2 is colored marker and colored pencil with white pencil highlights.

Plate 80. Contemporary-style display space. Medium is colored marker and colored pencil with white pencil highlights.

Medium in version 2 is pen and ink.

Plate 81. Transitional-style display space

Medium in version 1 is pen and ink with "cool" neutral marker figures to define human scale.

Plate 82. Transitional-style display space. Medium is pen and ink, colored marker, colored pencil with white pencil/ acrylic paint highlights, and "ghosting" in (dashed pen and ink lines) to represent table seating.

Plate 83. Transitional-style living space. Medium is colored marker, colored pencil with white pencil highlights, and "ghosting" in (dashed pen and ink lines) to represent piano in foreground.

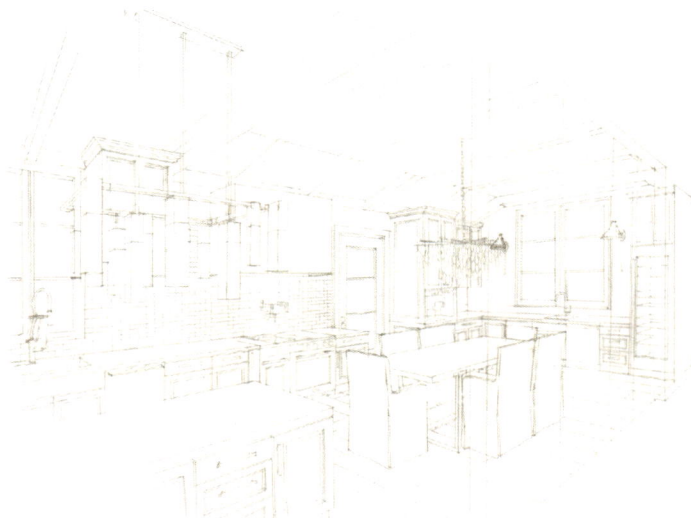

Preliminary pencil-line sketch, two-point perspective

Medium is colored marker, colored pencil, and
white pencil/acrylic paint highlights.

Plate 84. Modern farmhouse style

Preliminary pencil-line sketch, two-point perspective

Medium is colored marker, colored pencil, and
white pencil/acrylic paint highlights.

Plate 85. Modern farmhouse style—opposite view of plate 84

Plate 86. Contemporary-style memory loss facility atrium space. Medium is pen and ink, colored marker, colored pencil, and white pencil highlights.

Preliminary pen and ink, one-point perspective

Plate 87. Wrightian-style restaurant space. There is a play of geometric shapes in a vertical and/or horizontal relationship with the space, emphasizing "positive/negative" three dimensions.

Final presentation pen and ink, one-point perspective

Preliminary pen and ink, one-point perspective

Plate 88. Bungalow/Craftsman-style wedding venue. Medium is colored marker and colored pencil with white pencil/acrylic paint highlights, one-point perspective.

Two-point perspective of wedding venue ladies' room. Medium is colored marker and colored pencil with white pencil highlights.

Plate 89. Bungalow/Craftsman-style gathering venue version of plate 88. Preliminary is pen and ink, one-point perspective.

Plate 90. Bungalow/Craftsman-style gathering venue version of plate 89. Medium is pen and ink, colored marker and colored pencil with white pencil/acrylic paint highlights, one-point perspective.

Plate 91. French Eclectic-style stairwell. Medium is pen and ink, one-point perspective.

Plate 92. Contemporary industrial-style restaurant/bar. Medium is pen and ink, one-point perspective.

Plate 93. Contemporary Southwest-style living/dining areas. Medium is color marker, color pencil with white pencil highlights on manila cardstock, 2-point perspective

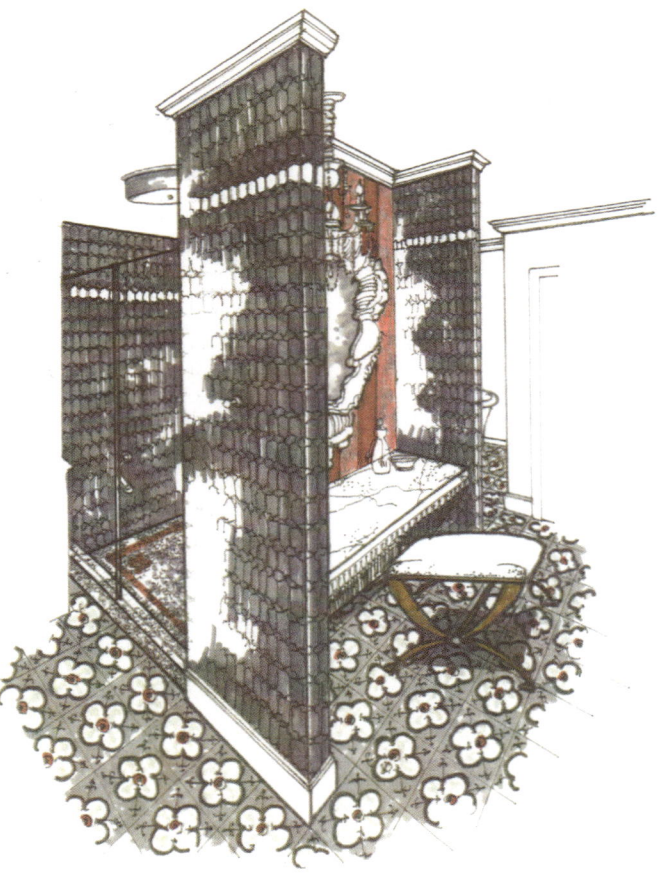

Plate 94. American Victorian-style hotel bathroom suite. Medium is pen and ink and colored marker, two-point perspective.

Outside seating view. Medium is pen and ink, colored marker, and colored pencil, two-point perspective.

View 1. Medium is pen and ink, colored marker, and colored pencil, two-point perspective.

Plate 95. Bungalow/Craftsman-style café

View 2. Medium is pen and ink, colored marker, and colored pencil, 2-point perspective.

Preliminary pen and ink, one-point perspective

Plate 96. Art moderne-style hotel suite. Medium is pen and ink, colored marker, and colored pencil with white pencil highlights, one-point perspective.

Plate 97. Art moderne-style hotel suite. Medium is pen and ink, two-point perspective.

two-point perspective

two-point perspective

Plate 98. Art moderne-style hotel suites. Medium is pen and ink.

two-point perspective

two-point perspective

Preliminary pen and ink, 1-point perspective

Plate 99. Traditional-style hotel suite. Medium is pen and ink, colored marker, and colored pencil with white pencil highlights, one-point perspective.

Preliminary pen and ink, two-point perspective

Plate 100. Art deco-style gathering room. Medium is pen and ink, colored marker, and colored pencil with white pencil highlights, two-point perspective.

Preliminary pen and ink, 2-point perspective

Plate 101. Art deco-style gathering room. Medium is pen and ink, colored marker, and colored pencil with white pencil highlights, two-point perspective.

Preliminary pen and ink, one-point perspective

Plate 102. Art deco-style gathering room. Medium is pen and ink, colored marker, and colored pencil with white pencil/acrylic paint highlights, one-point perspective.

Preliminary pen and ink, two-point perspective

Plate 103. Contemporary Southwest-style café. Medium is pen and ink, colored marker, and colored pencil with white pencil/acrylic paint highlights, two-point perspective.

Plate 104. Art deco-style restaurant bar. Medium is pen and ink, two-point perspective.

Plate 105. Art deco-style restaurant bar. Medium is pen and ink, colored marker, and colored pencil with white pencil/acrylic paint highlights, two-point perspective.

Plate 106. Art deco-style restaurant. Medium is pen and ink, two-point perspective.

Plate 107. Art deco-style restaurant. Medium is pen and ink, colored marker, and color pencil with white pencil/acrylic paint highlights, two-point perspective.

Version 2. Medium is pen and ink and colored marker/colored pencil with white pencil and acrylic paint highlights, two-point perspective.

Plate 109. Contemporary-style guest bath version 1. Medium is pen and ink and colored marker/colored pencil with white pencil and acrylic paint highlights, two-point perspective.

Plate 108. American Victorian-style library. Medium is pen and ink, one-point perspective.

Plate 110. Contemporary-style: kitchen. Medium is colored marker/colored pencil with white pencil and acrylic paint highlights, two-point perspectives.

Transitional style. Medium is pen and ink, two-point perspective.

Transitional style. Medium is pen and ink, two-point perspective.

Transitional style. Medium is pen and ink, two-point perspective.

Contemporary Southwest-style. Medium is pen and ink, two-point perspective.

Plate 111. Various styles in pen and ink.

Bar. Medium is watercolor with colored-pencil highlighting, two-point perspective.

Living/solarium. Medium is watercolor with colored-pencil highlighting, two-point perspective.

Kitchen. Medium is watercolor with colored-pencil highlighting, two-point perspective.

Plate 112. Contemporary Southwest-style home design

Plate 113. Contemporary Southwest-style solarium. Medium is watercolor with colored-pencil highlighting, two-point perspective.

Plate 114. Contemporary-style master bedroom. Medium is watercolor with colored-pencil highlighting, one-point perspective.

Plate 115. Contemporary-style country club dining room. Medium is watercolor with colored-pencil highlighting, one-point perspective.

Preliminary pencil drawing, two-point perspective

Plate 116. Contemporary-style kitchen. Medium is colored marker and colored pencil with white-pencil/acrylic-paint highlighting, two-point perspective.

Preliminary pencil drawing,
one-point perspective

Plate 117. Contemporary-style kitchen. Medium is colored marker and colored pencil with white-pencil/acrylic-paint highlighting, one-point perspective.

Preliminary pencil drawing, one-point "birds-eye" perspective

Plate 118. Contemporary-style kitchen. Medium is colored marker and colored pencil with white-pencil/acrylic-paint highlighting, one-point "birds-eye" perspective.

Preliminary pencil drawing, two-point perspective

Plate 119. Modern farmhouse-style kitchen. Medium is colored marker, colored
pencil, and white-pencil/acrylic-paint highlighting, two-point perspective.

Preliminary pen and ink, one-point perspective

Plate 120. Contemporary-style kitchen, late evening view. Medium is colored marker and colored pencil with white-pencil/acrylic-paint highlighting, one-point perspective.

Preliminary pen and ink, 2-point perspective

Plate 121. Contemporary-style kitchen. Medium is colored marker, colored pencil, and white-pencil/acrylic-paint highlighting, two-point perspective.

Preliminary pen and ink, one-point perspective

Plate 122. Contemporary-style kitchen. Medium is colored marker, colored pencil, and white-pencil/acrylic-paint highlighting, one-point perspective.

Preliminary pen and ink, one-point perspective

Plate 123. Traditional-style kitchen. Medium is colored marker, colored pencil, and white-pencil/acrylic-paint highlighting, one-point perspective.

Preliminary pen and ink, one-point perspective

Plate 124. Contemporary-style kitchen. Medium is colored marker, colored pencil, and white-pencil/acrylic-paint highlighting, one-point perspective.

Preliminary pen and ink, one-point perspective

Plate 125. Contemporary-style kitchen. Medium is colored marker, colored pencil, and white-pencil/acrylic-paint highlighting, one-point perspective.

Preliminary pen and ink,
two-point perspective

Plate 126. Contemporary-style kitchen. Medium is colored marker, colored
pencil, and white-pencil/acrylic-paint highlighting, two-point perspective.

Plate 127. Contemporary-style kitchen. Medium is colored marker, colored pencil, and white-pencil/acrylic-paint highlighting, one-point "bird's-eye" perspective of plate 120.

Section 6

Floor Plans and Site Plans

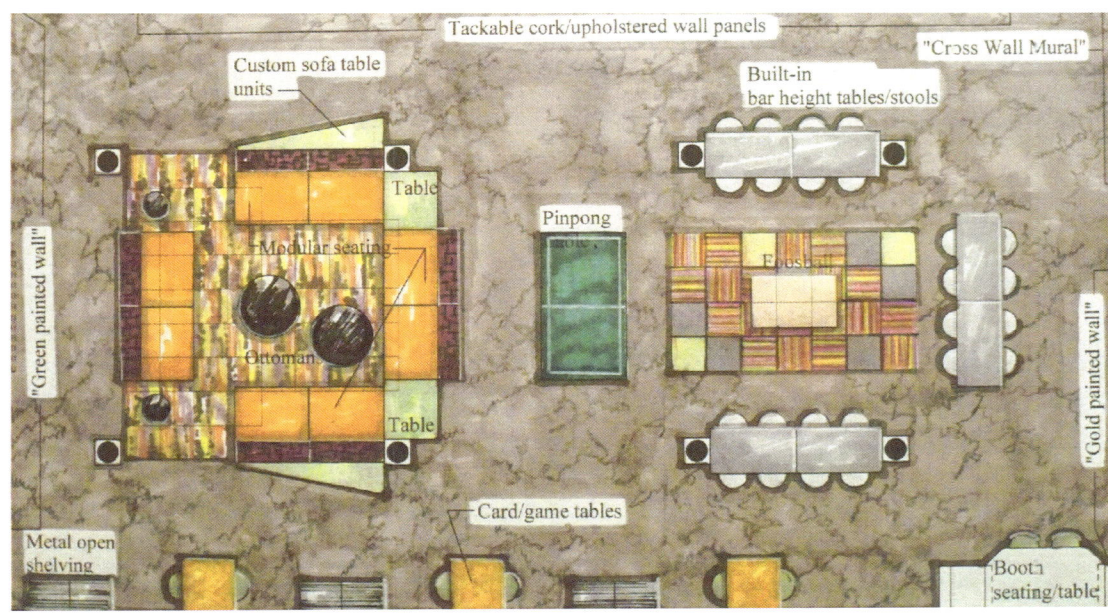

Plate 128. Contemporary-style game room. Medium is colored marker, colored pencil, and white pencil highlights.

Plate 129. Contemporary-style great room. Medium is colored marker, colored pencil, and white pencil highlights.

Plate 130. Traditional-style great room. Medium is colored marker, colored pencil, and white pencil highlights.

Plate 131. Traditional-style sitting room. Medium is colored marker, colored pencil, and white pencil highlights.

Plate 132. Contemporary-style sitting room. Medium is colored marker, colored pencil, and white pencil/acrylic paint highlights, one-point "bird's-eye" perspective view.

Plate 133. Generic rendered plan. Medium is colored marker, colored pencil, and white pencil highlights.

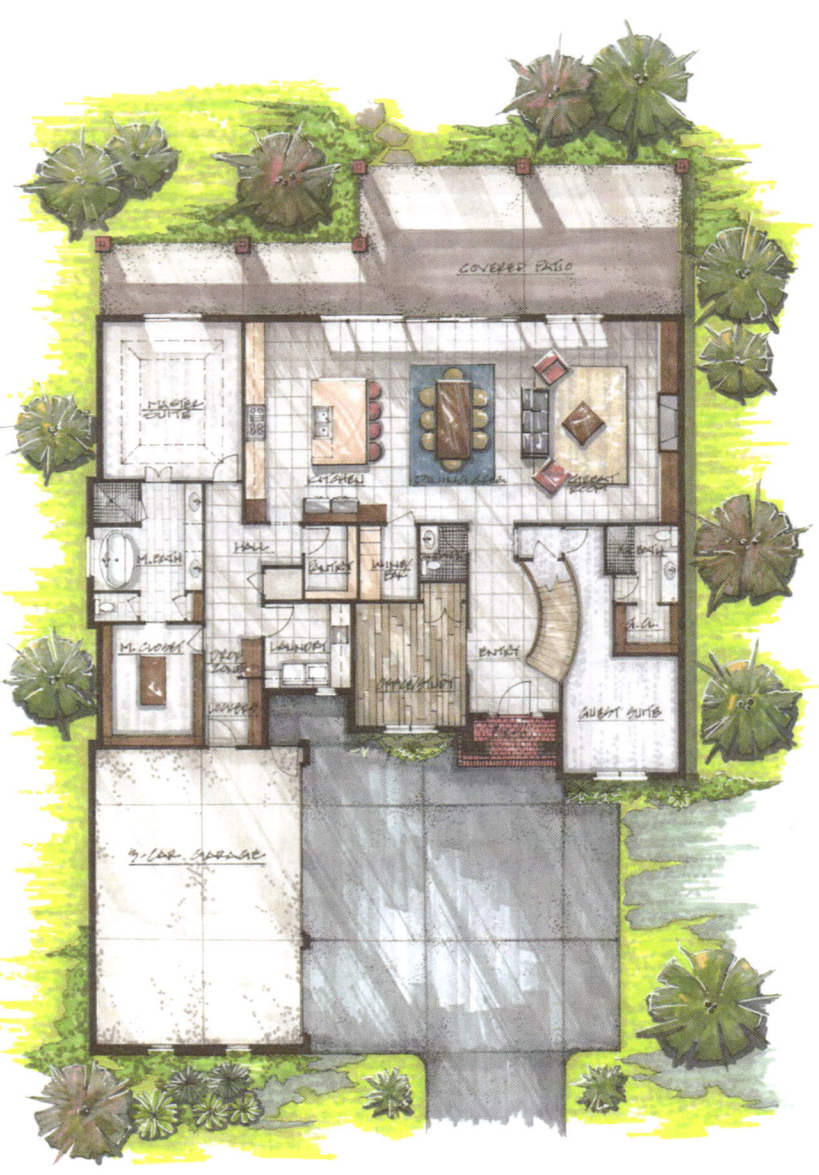

Plate 134. Rendered plan with contemporary-style theme. Medium us colored marker, colored pencil, and white pencil/acrylic paint highlights.

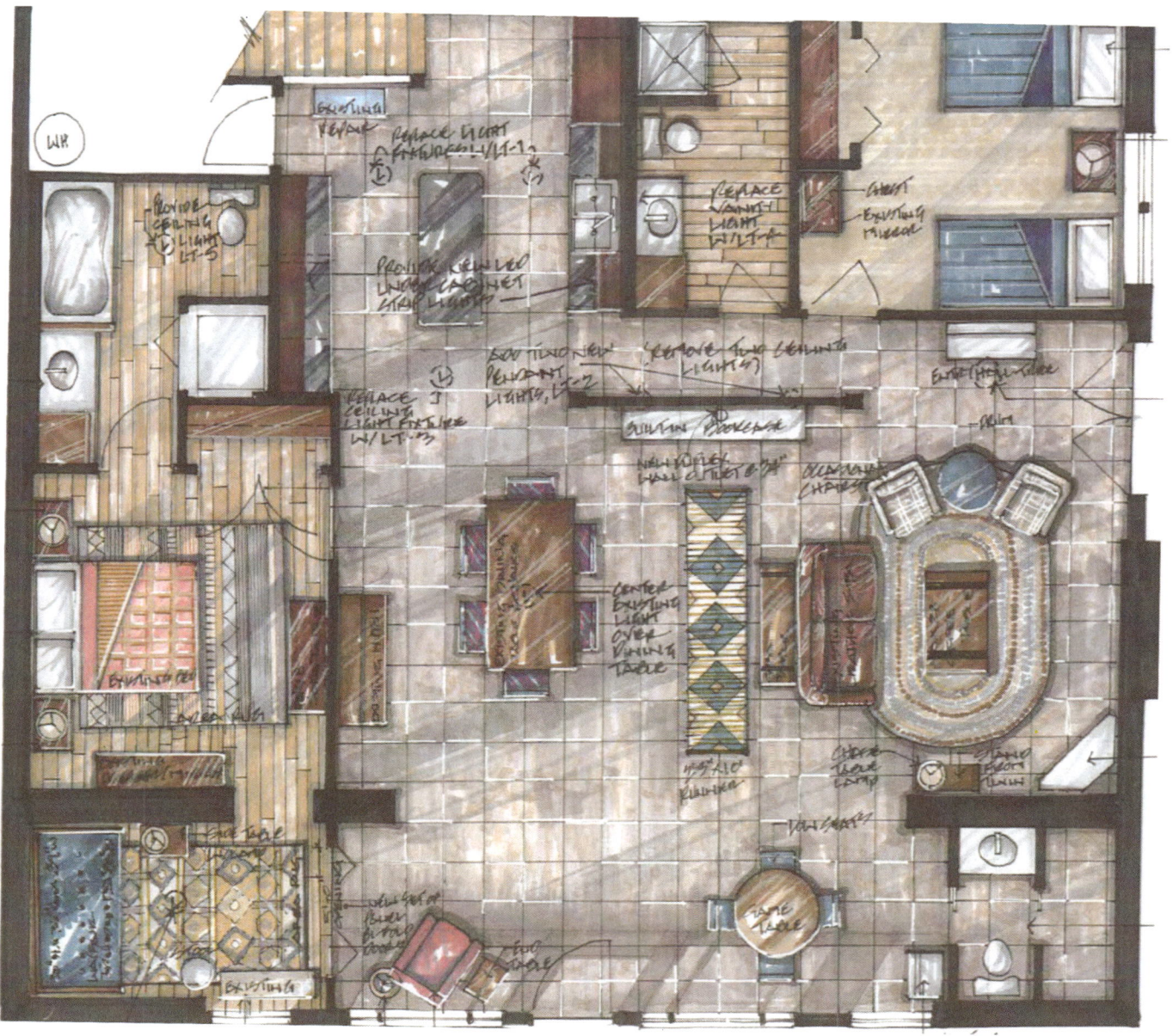

Plate 135. Rendered floor plan. Medium is colored marker, colored pencil, and white pencil/acrylic paint highlights.

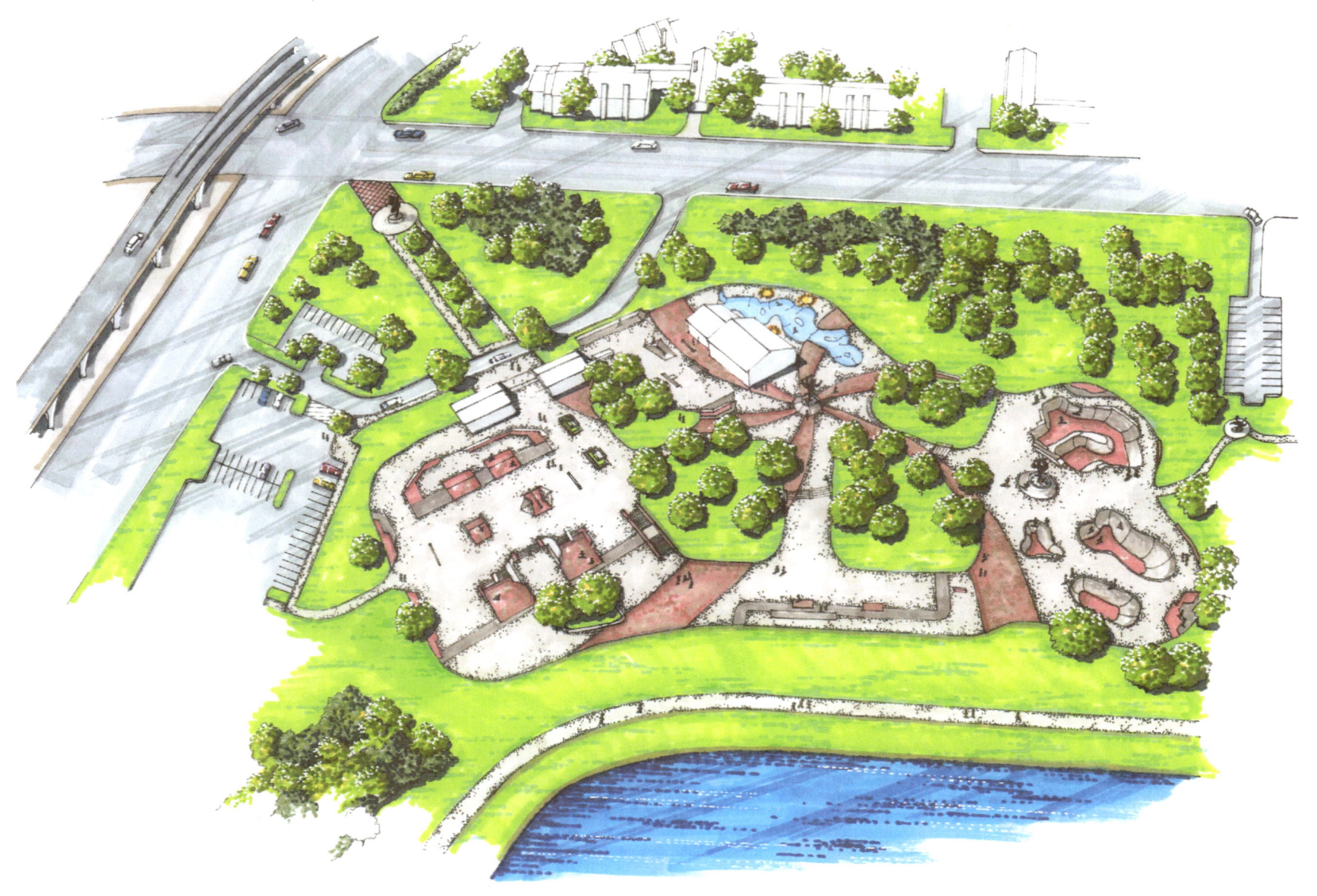

Plate 136. Rendered 3D plan oblique of skateboard park. Medium is colored marker, colored pencil, and white pencil/acrylic paint highlights.

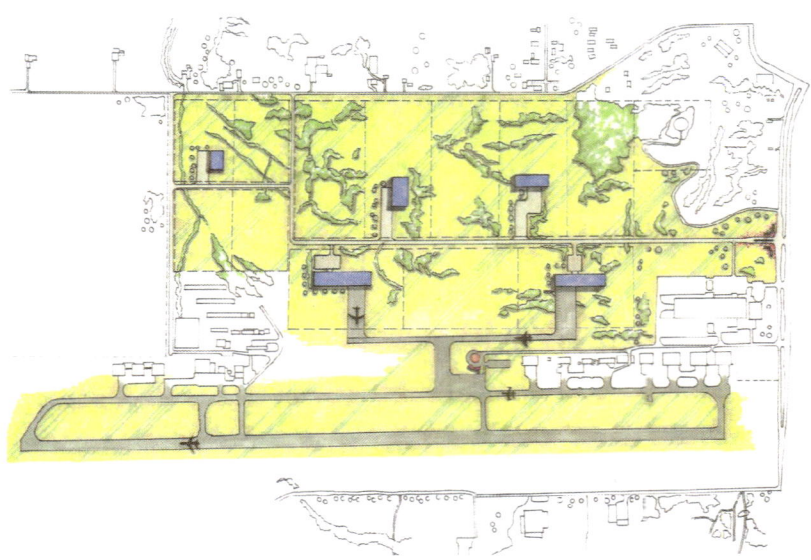

Plate 137. Rendered site plan of a regional airport. Medium is colored marker, colored pencil, and white pencil highlights.

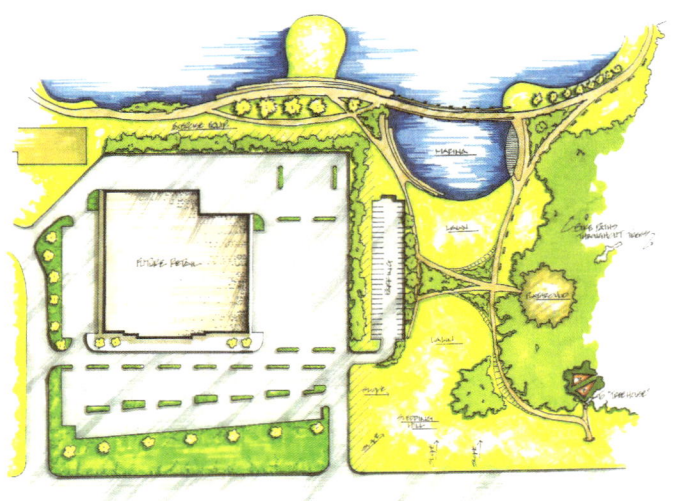

Plate 138. Rendered site plan of a retail center. Medium is colored marker, colored pencil, and white pencil highlights.

Plate 139. Rendered site plan of a "historical walkway." Medium is colored marker, colored pencil, and white pencil/acrylic paint highlights.

Section 7

Furnishings

Plate 140. Contemporary Southwest-style screen. Medium is colored marker with pen-and-ink highlighting.

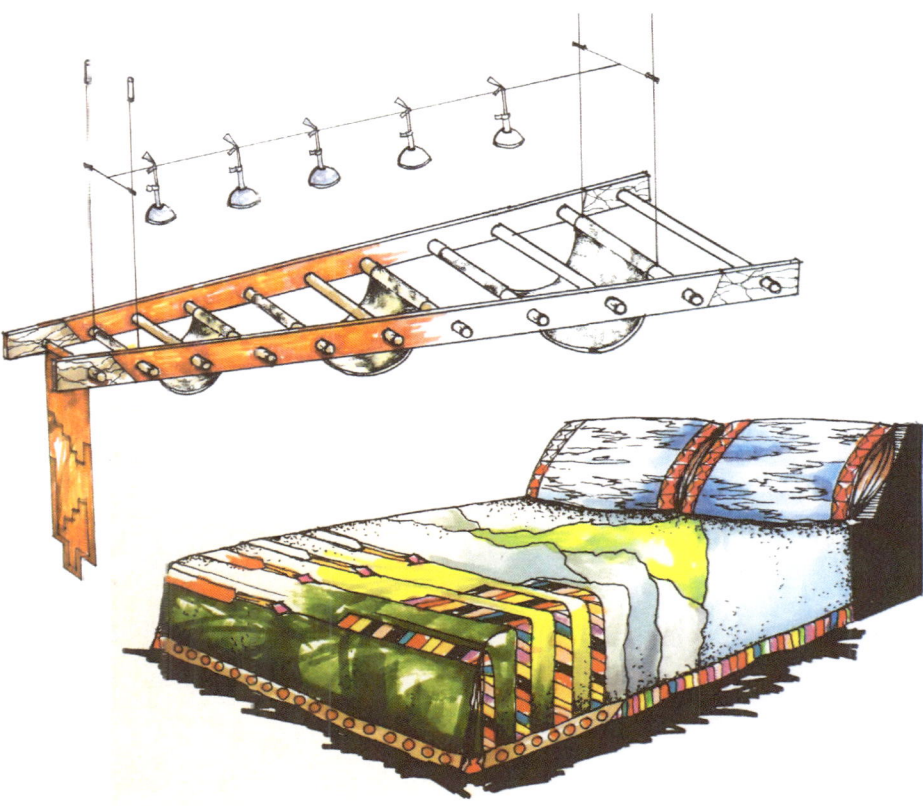

Plate 141. Contemporary Southwest-style bed. Medium is colored marker with pen-and-ink highlighting.

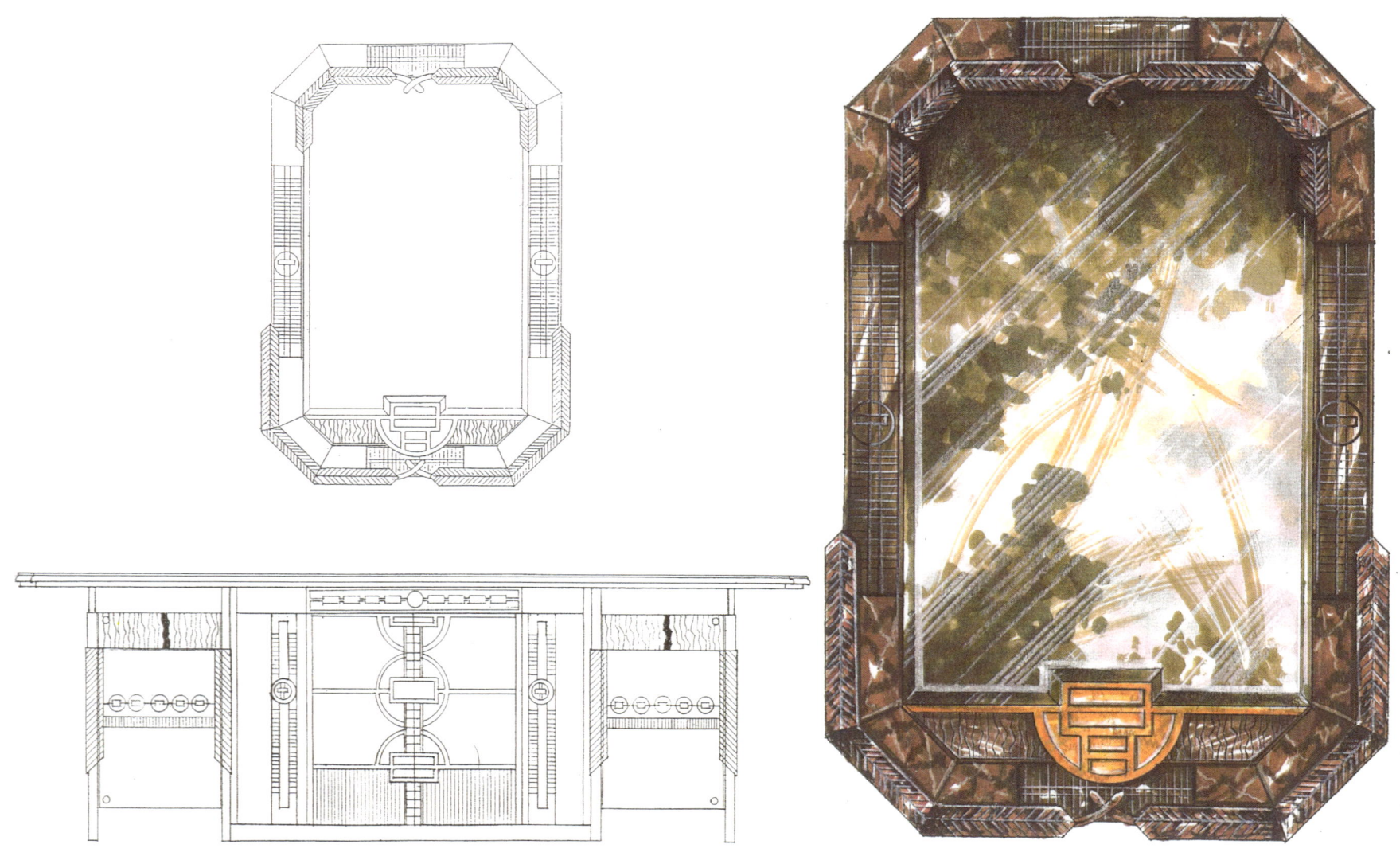

Plate 143. Contemporary Southwest-style sofa table and mirror. Medium is colored marker with white-pencil highlighting.

Plate 145. Contemporary neoclassical-style display table. Medium is colored marker with white-pencil highlighting.

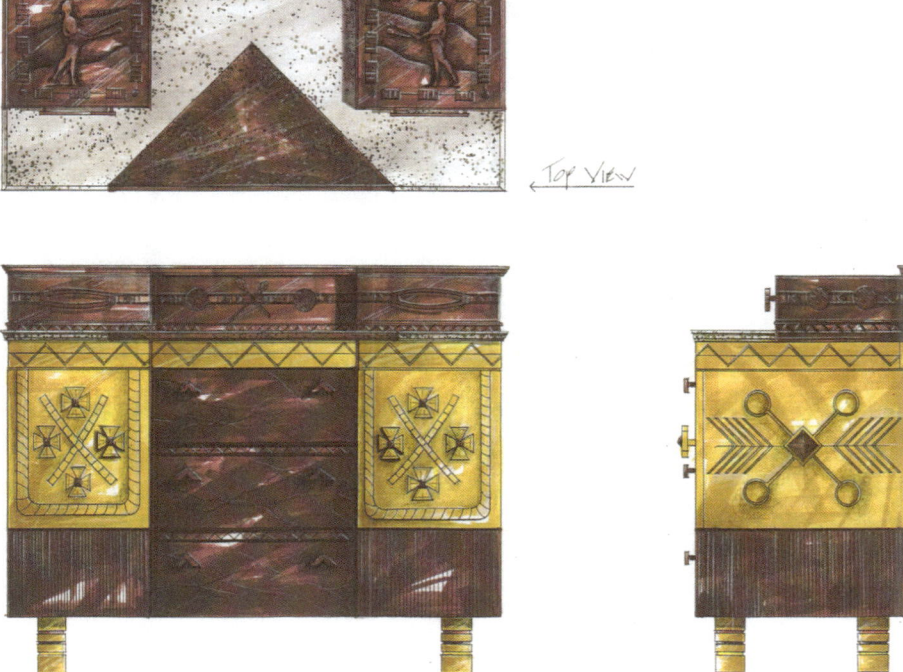

Top View

Plate 144. Contemporary Native American-style buffet from the author's Native Lines Collection. Medium is colored marker with white-pencil highlighting.

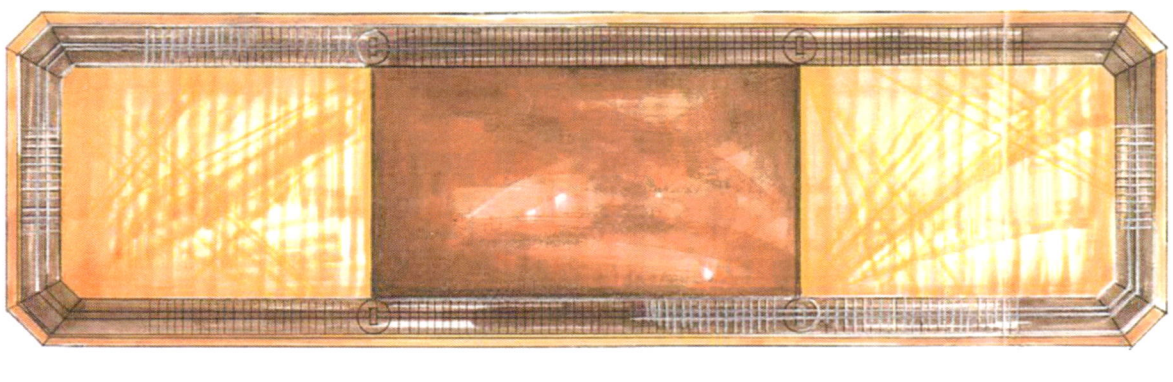

TOP VIEW

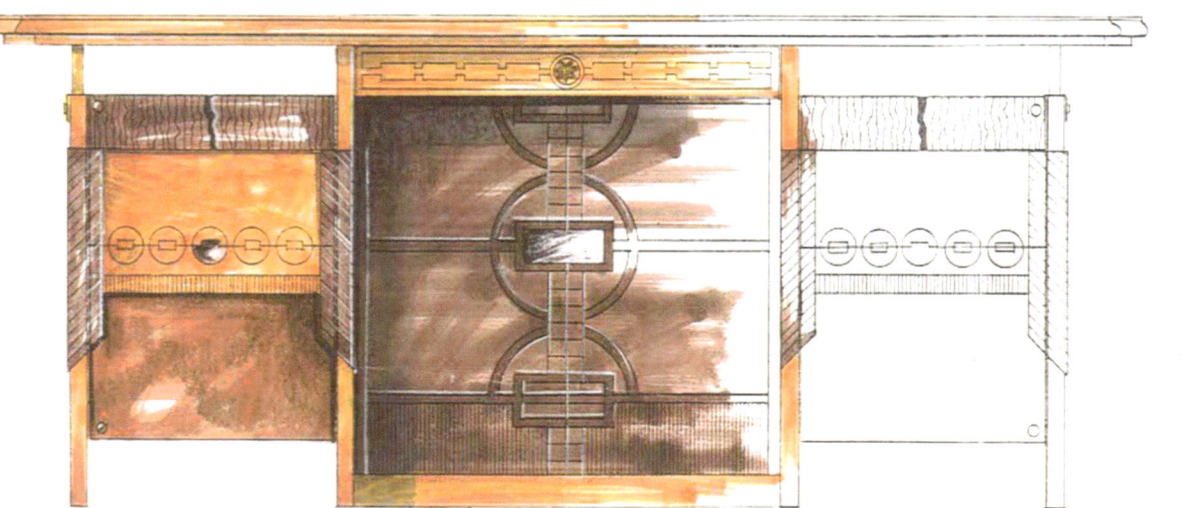

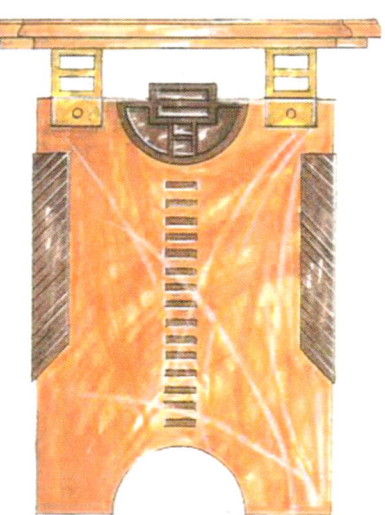

Plate 146. Contemporary Southwest-style credenza. Medium is colored marker with white-pencil highlighting.

Plate 147. Contemporary Native American-style display towers from the author's Native Lines
Collection. Medium is colored marker with white-pencil highlighting.

TOP LID VIEW

Plate 148. Contemporary Native American-style blanket chest from the author's Native Lines Collection. Medium is colored marker with white-pencil highlighting.

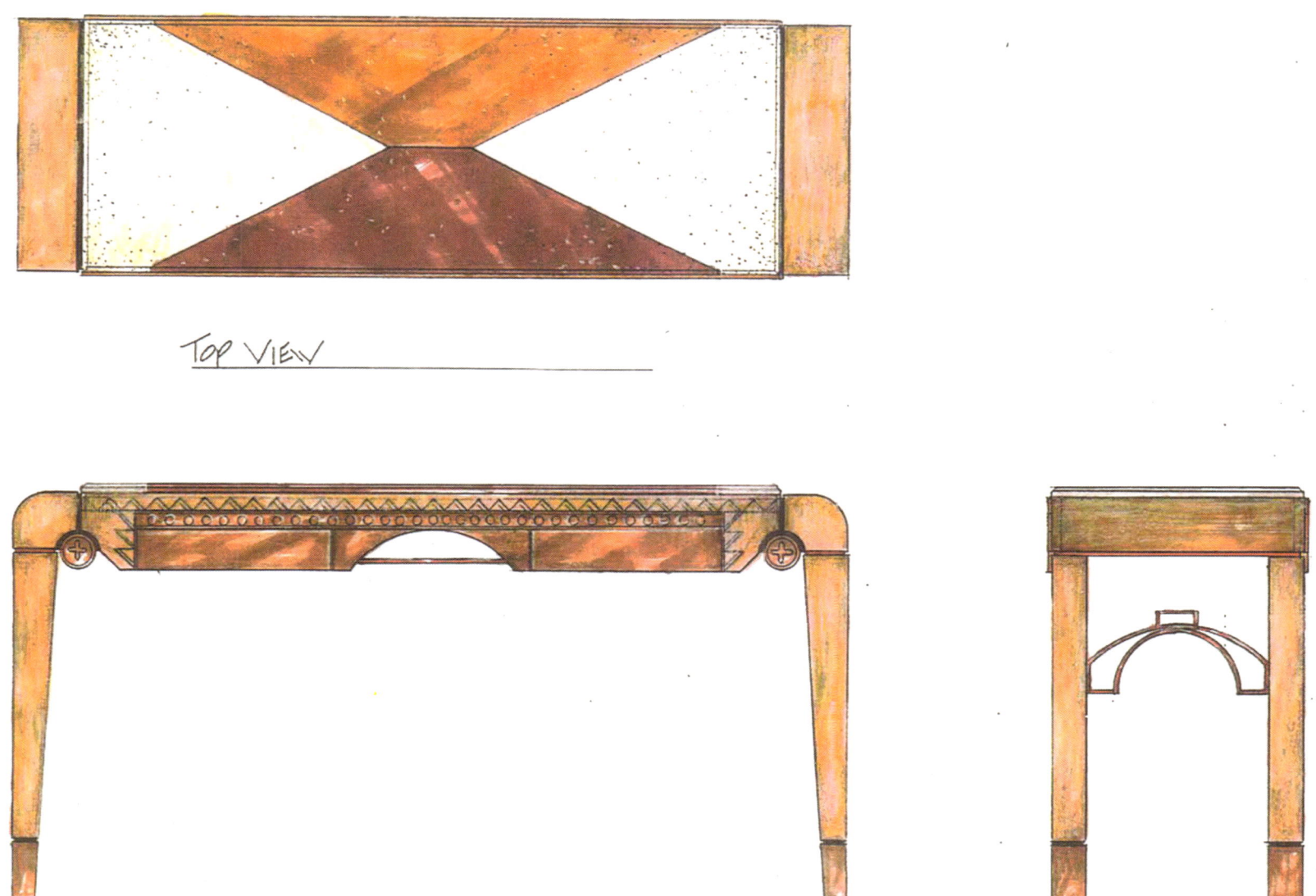

TOP VIEW

Plate 149. Contemporary Native American-style sofa table from the author's Native Lines
Collection. Medium is colored marker with white-pencil highlighting.

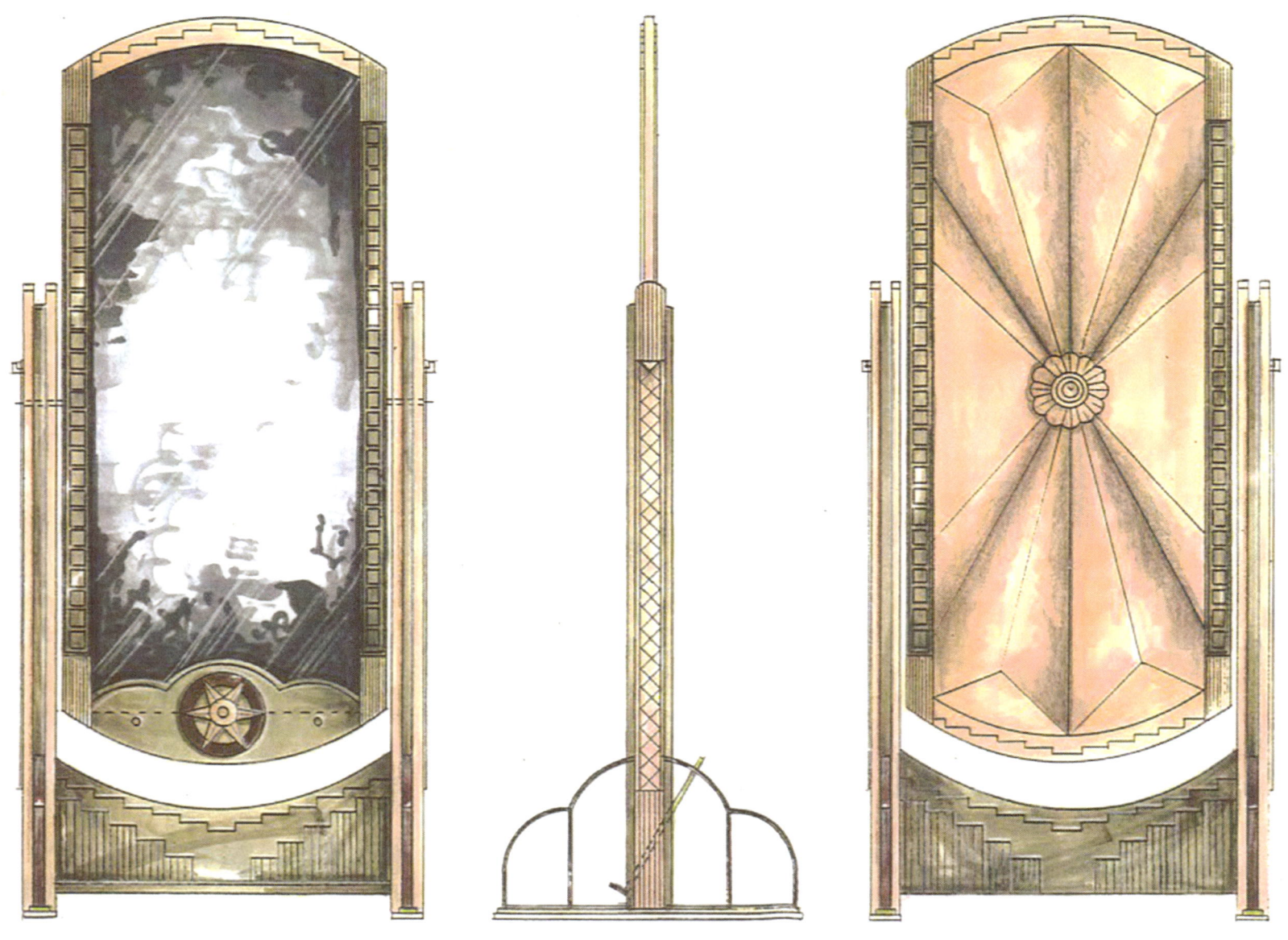

Plate 150. Contemporary Native American-style floor mirror from the author's Native Lines Collection. Medium is colored marker with white-pencil highlighting.

Plate 151. Contemporary-style four-poster bed. Medium is colored
marker with white-pencil/acrylic-paint highlighting.

Plate 152. Contemporary-style coffee table.
Medium is colored marker with white-
pencil/acrylic-paint highlighting.

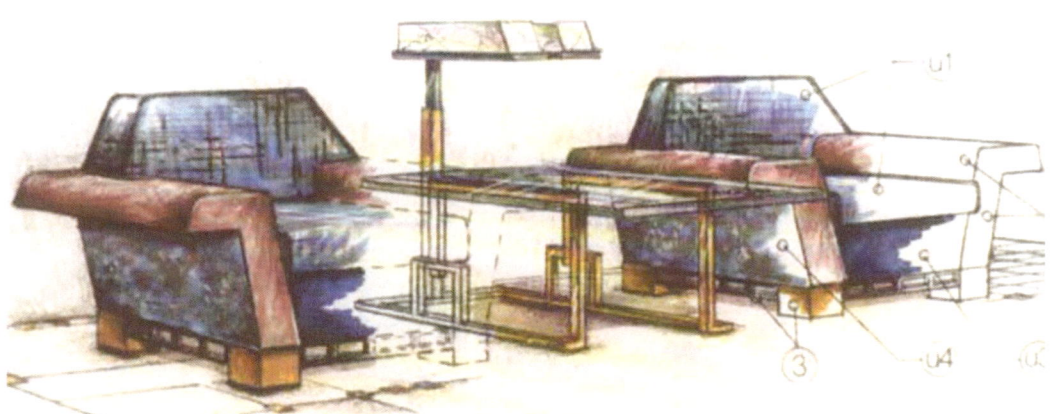

Plate 153. Art deco-style lounge chairs and occasional table/lamp.
Medium is colored marker with white-pencil highlighting.

Plate 154. American Victorian-style vanity. Medium:
colored marker with white-pencil highlighting.

Plate 155. Art deco-style love seat sofa. Medium is
colored marker with white-pencil highlighting.

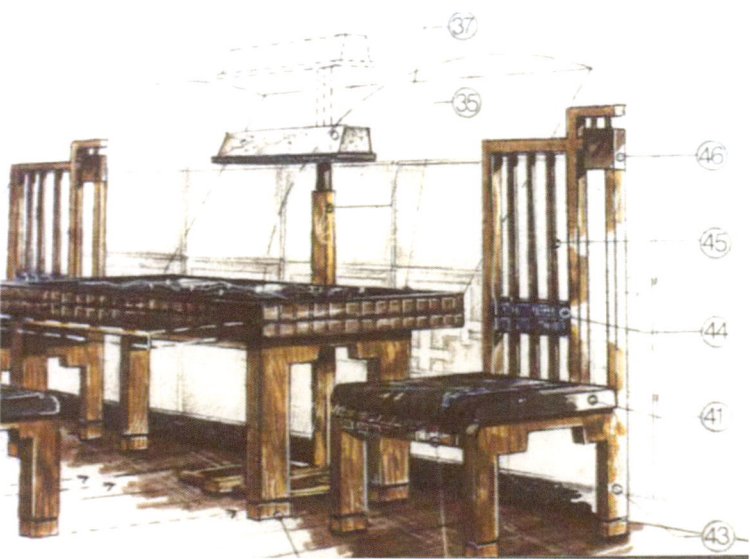

Plate 156. Art deco-style side chairs and table/lamp. Medium
is colored marker with white-pencil highlighting.

Plate 157. Contemporary-style TV cabinet. Medium is colored marker with white-pencil highlighting.

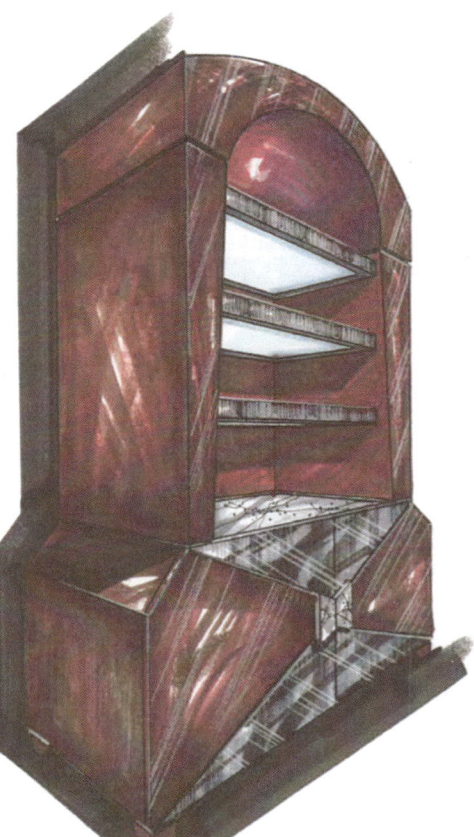

Plate 158. Contemporary-style hutch. Medium is colored marker with white-pencil highlighting.

Plate 159. Contemporary-style credenza. Medium is colored marker with white-pencil highlighting.

Copyright-Free Line Drawings

"Enjoy Color Rendering"

Plate 160

Plate 161

Plate 162

Plate 163

Plate 164

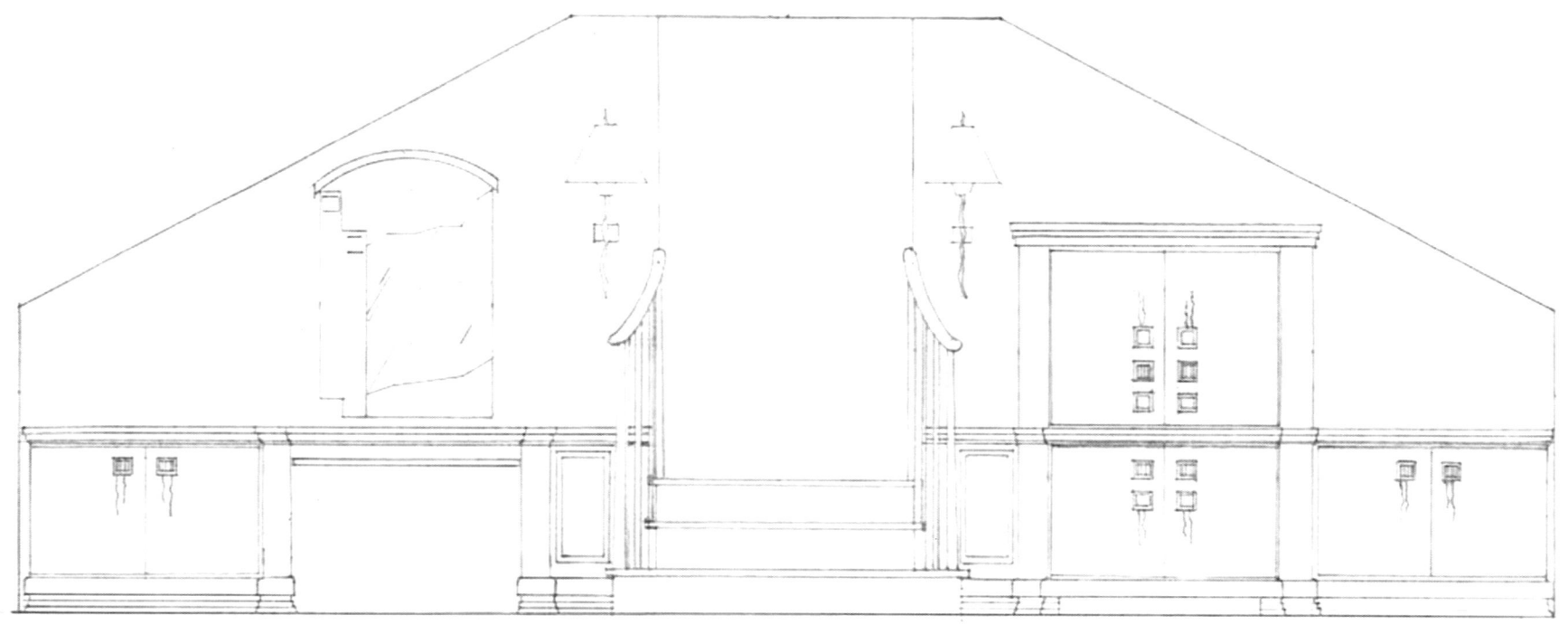

Plate 165

Plate 166

Plate 167

Plate 163

Plate 169

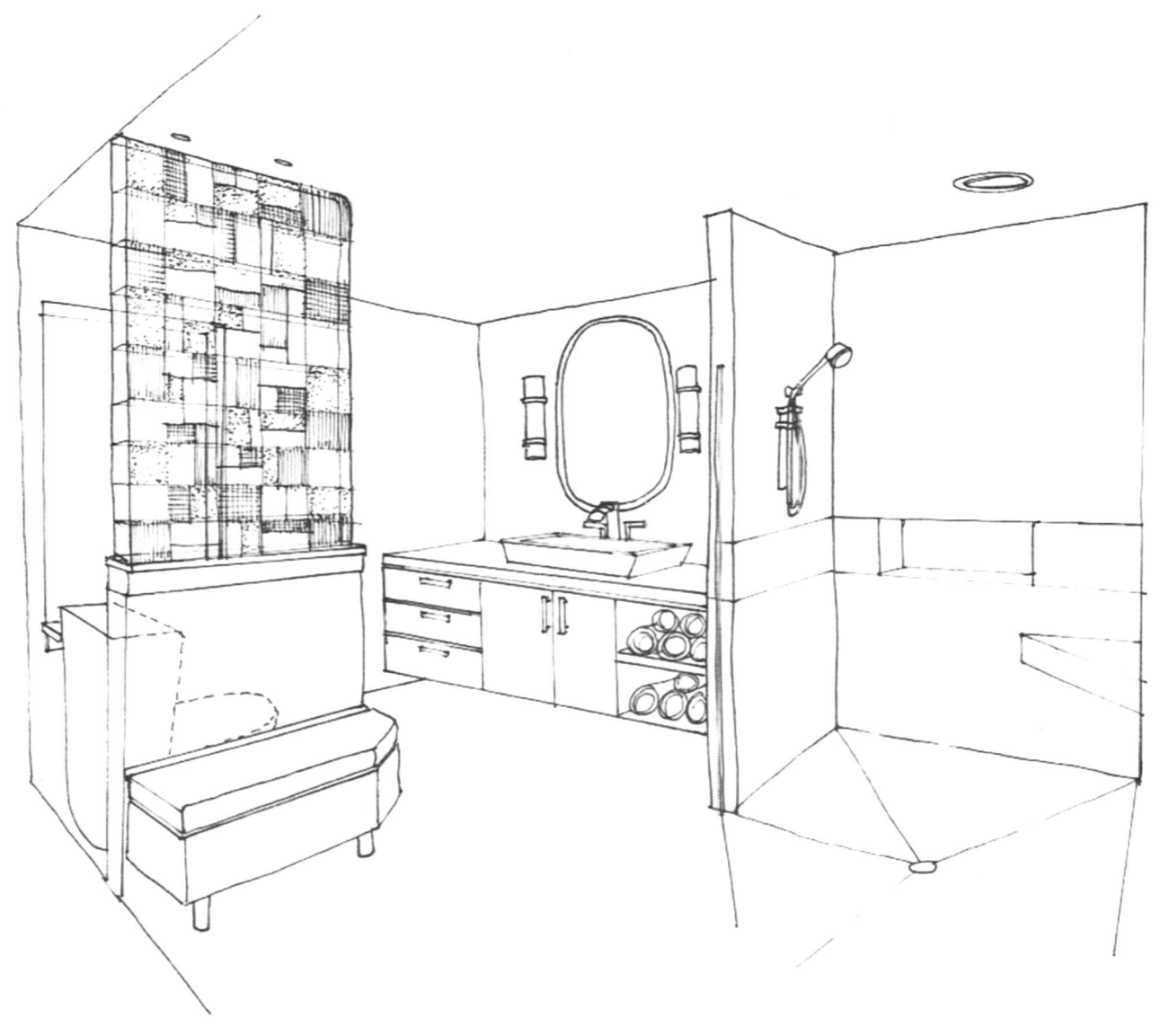

Plate 170

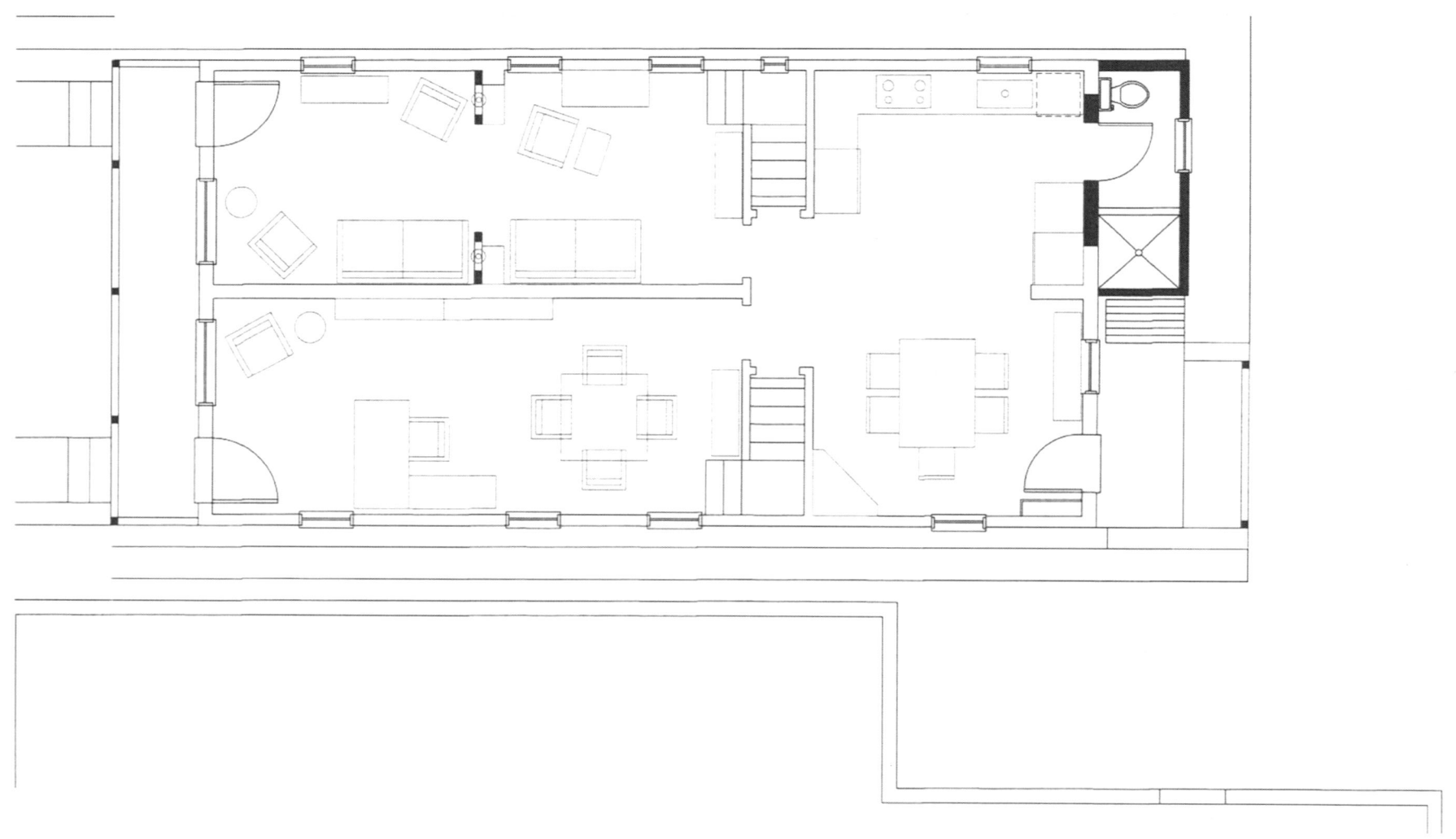

Plate 171

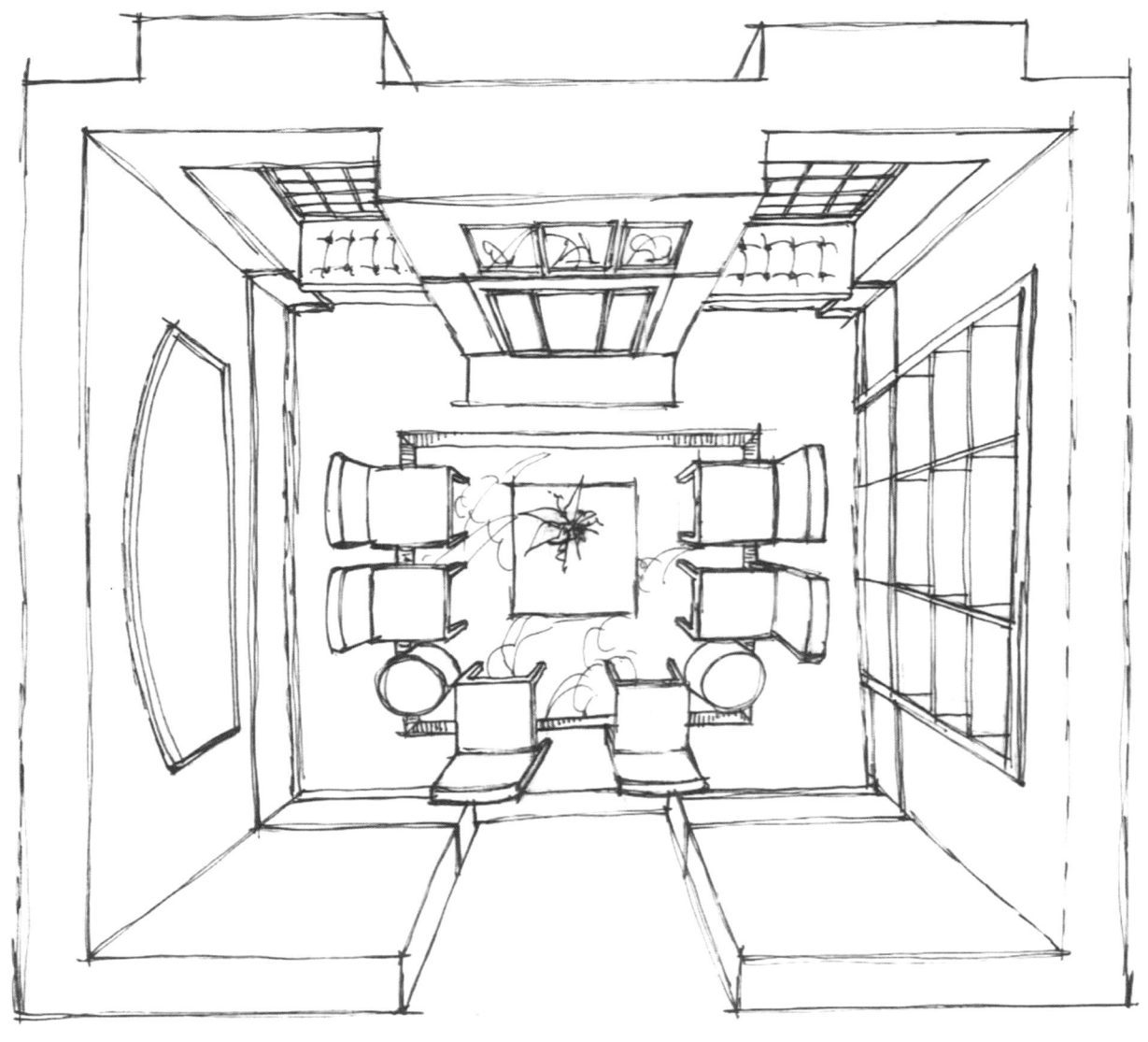

Plate 172

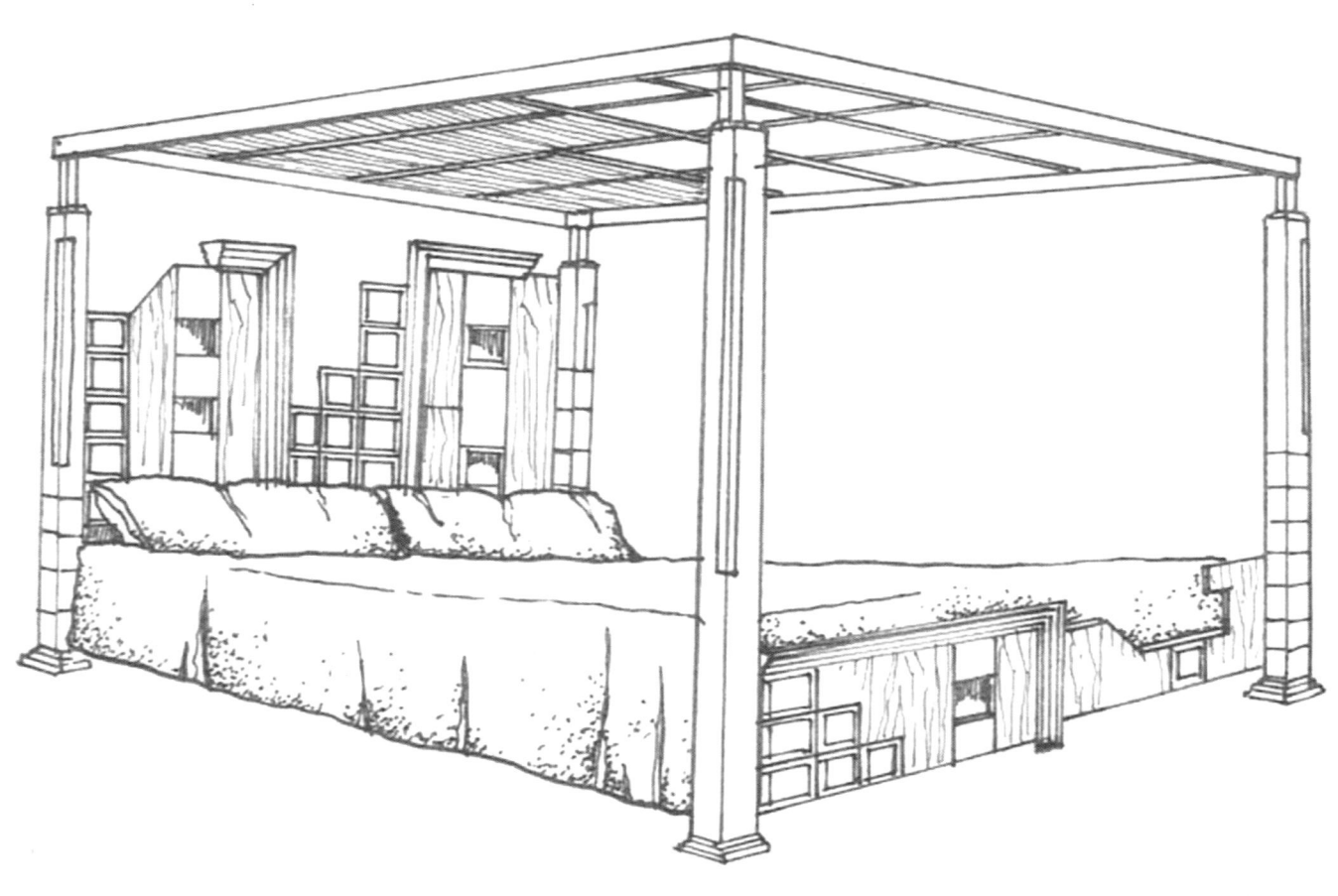

Plate 173

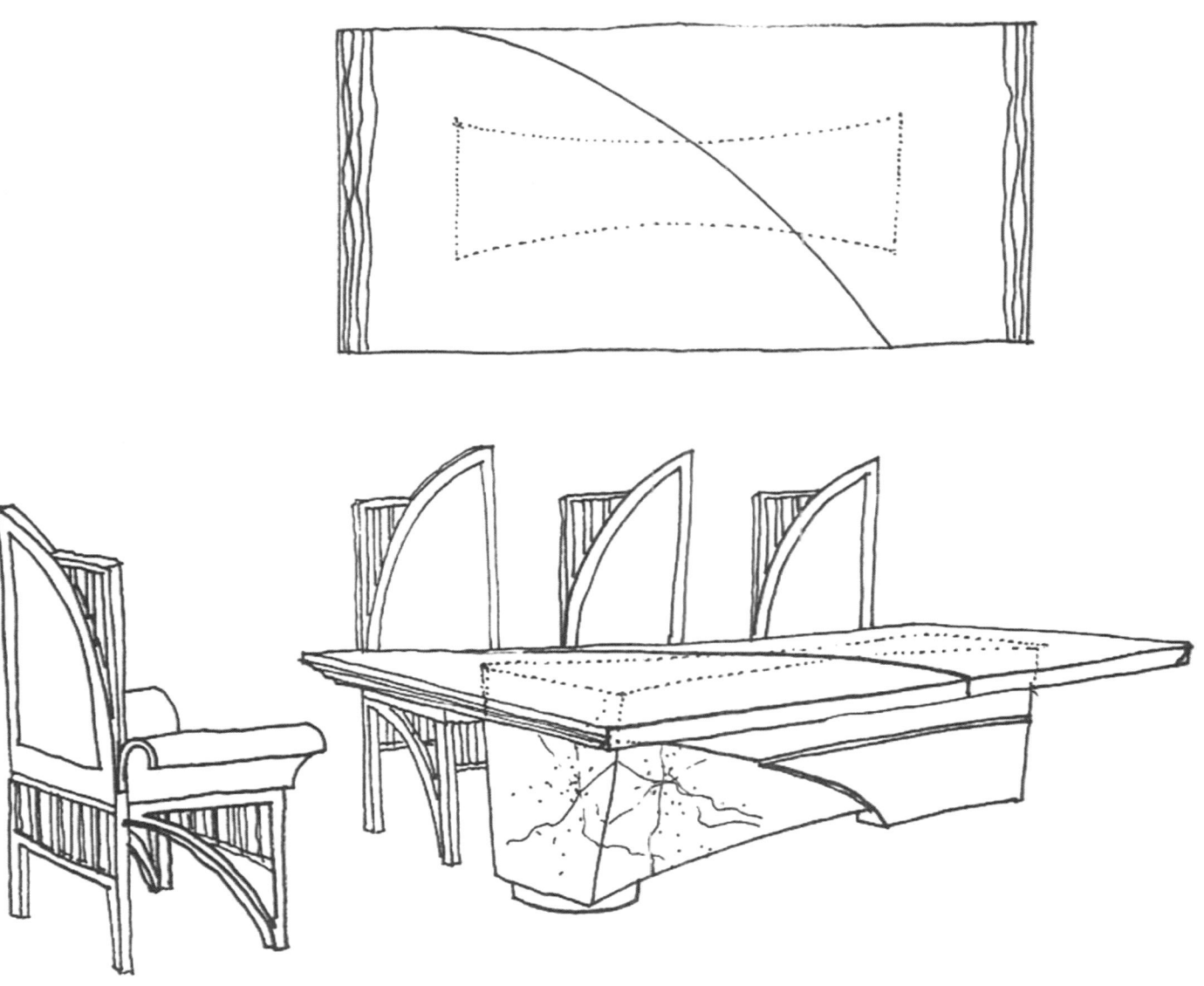

Plate 174

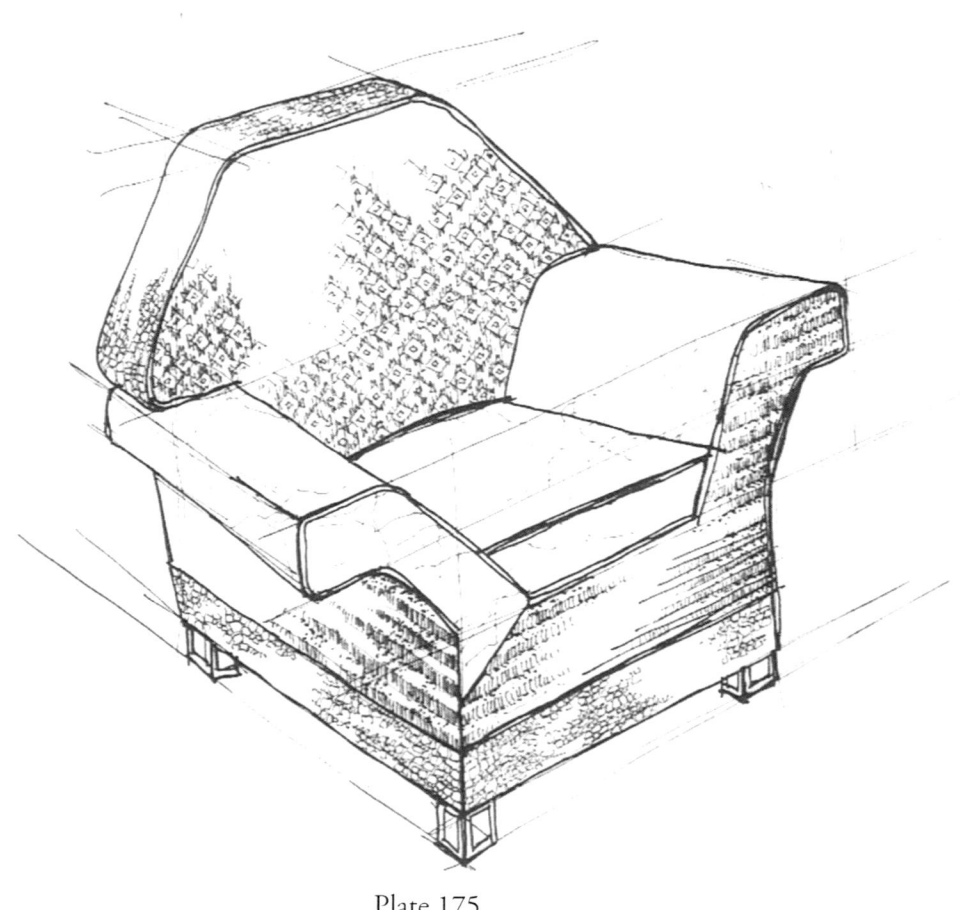

Plate 175

Illustration Credits

The author wishes to acknowledge and thank the following visionaries and support in creating rendered illustrations for their endeavors in the built environment.

Ambler Architects, plates 55, 56, 57 (Kiddie Park entry gate and Woolaroc building exterior), 58 (OKU athletic facility), 80 (Price Tower exhibit hall celebrating the 150th birthday of Frank Lloyd Wright), 87 (Copper Restaurant, Price Tower), 88 (Woolaroc gathering place), 89, 90, 92, 94, 95, 103, 136, 137 (Woolaroc gathering place).

Bainbridge Design Group, plates 1, 2, 3, 4, 5, 6, 7, 8, 9, 10, 11, 12, 13, 25, 26.

Brian D. Wiggs Homes, Inc., plates 24, 41, 52, 53, 73, 74, 75, 76, 77, 78, 79, 91, 100, 101, 102.

Customs by Vaughn, plates 57 (bottom left, top right), 58 (top left, top right), 138.

Duvall Atelier, plates 104, 105, 106, 107.

Ferrell Building Products, plate 27.

George Beltz, plate 134.

Henk-Seng Design, LLC, plate 96

Jamie Birks, plates 39, 40.

Jane Swinney, plate 152.

Jerald Vahn Willis Designs, plate 111 (top left and right, bottom left).

Joe Alcott, plate 70.

June Worthington, plates 112, 113, 114.

Kitchen Concepts, plates 84, 85, 98 (bottom right), 108, 110, 154.

Kappa Kappa Iota, plate 50.

KKT Architects, Inc., plate 58 (lower left).

KSQ Design, plate 54.

Liz and Fred Hegenbart, plate 109.

Mel Bean Interiors, plate 83.

Merritt Properties, plate 31.

Nex Gen Builders, plates 22, 23.

New Line Skateparks, Inc., plate 136.

SKS (Signature Kitchen Suites), plates 65 (except for upper left), 66, 67 (except for upper right), 116, 117, 118, 119, 120, 121, 122, 123, 124, 125, 126, 127.

Steve White, plate 29.

Suanne Blair, plates 42, 43, 44.

Tom Little, plate 51.

WSB Homes, plates 17, 133, 134.

About the Author

The author is a retired interior designer and professor of interior design from Oklahoma State University with a bachelor of architecture and master of science degrees (interior design) from Oklahoma State University. His area of specialization has been furniture design and presentation illustration as well as conducting sketching and color rendering workshops across the country. He has a copyrighted furniture collection inspired by Native American history and culture and exhibited these works in gallery showrooms in Oklahoma, Arizona, New Mexico, New York, Houston, and Chicago. Rick was also a design consultant for a national retail fixture and furnishings manufacturer.

He currently creates hand-drawn pen-and-ink and colored renderings (marker and watercolor) for architects, designers, builders, and personal clients such as exterior 2D and 3D home portraits, conceptual building illustrations, and various interior 2D and 3D drawings. The author obtains inspiration from Native American history, Frank Lloyd Wright, Georgia O'Keeffe, Nicolai Fechin, art deco, and contemporary design.

The author's decision to create and publish a book such as this was at the request of former students and design professionals of sharing his illustration techniques as a visual source of inspiration and design ideas and to foster and preserve the art of hand-drawn rendering. Rick hopes that hand-drawn renderings of architecture and interior design will appeal to art-book enthusiasts as well. .

CPSIA information can be obtained
at www.ICGtesting.com
Printed in the USA
LVRC100006140521
687391LV00001B/1